9 between [bitwíːn]
（2つ）の間に

the distance **between** the two cities
2つの市の間の距離

10 among [əmʌ́ŋ]
（3つ以上）の間に

a singer **among** his fans
ファンに囲まれた歌手

11 in [ín]
〜の中に

students **in** the classroom
教室の中にいる生徒

12 into [íntə]
〜の中へ

come **into** the classroom
教室の中へ入ってくる

13 through [θrúː]
〜を通り抜けて

go **through** the tunnel
トンネルを通り抜ける

14 across [əkrɔ́ːs]
〜を横切って

swim **across** the river
川を泳いで渡る

15 along [əlɔ́ːŋ]
〜に沿って

shops **along** the street
通り沿いの店

16 toward [tɔ́ːrd]
〜の方へ

walk **toward** the window
窓の方へ歩く

ハイパー
英語教室

中学
英語長文2 改訂版
［入試長文がすらすら読める編］

東進ハイスクール中等部・
東進中学NET講師
大岩秀樹／

東進ハイスクール・
東進ビジネススクール講師
安河内哲也 著

桐原書店

はじめに

　英語は君が世界に出ていくためのパスポートです。世界中で君と同じ年齢の人たちが英語を勉強しています。日本だけでなく，アフリカでもアジアでもヨーロッパでも，みんな英語を勉強しているのです。そして，**英語を使ってさまざまな国の人たちがコミュニケーション**をとっています。

　さて，英語を学ぶ上で身につけなければならないことはいくつかありますが，その１つは**英文を読めるようになることです**。今は新聞や本，そしてインターネットを通して世界中の出来事を知ることができます。その記事の多くは英語で書かれているので，英語が読めれば世界中の出来事をすばやく知ることができるのです。これは将来，世界で活躍する君にとって**絶対に必要な力**ですよね。

　この本では，高校入試で出題された英語長文を通して，**英文の読み方を**学びます。英文を読むときは，作者が何を伝えようとしているのか，そのメッセージを読み取ろうとしてください。何よりも，英文を味わおうという気持ちを持つことが大切です。

　この本では，どんな人にでも**楽しく，わかりやすく，スッキリ**と理解できるように解説していきますから，英語が苦手な人も安心してくださいね。

　そして理解したあとは，音声を使って，学んだ英文を**音読**しましょう。**何も見なくても言えるくらい何度も音読することが，語学習得の一番の近道**です。英語もスポーツや音楽と同様に，**楽しんでやると早くマスターで**きます。

　音読は机でやる必要はありません。**好きな場所で，好きなポーズで，心をこめて音読**しましょう。
　君は必ず英語ができるようになります。

2021年 初夏　大岩秀樹／安河内哲也

Contents

はじめに 2
本書の構成と効果的な使い方 4

Unit 1 8
説明文／英語の学習

Unit 2 14
物語／ベンジャミン・フランクリン

Unit 3 20
エッセイ／記憶

Unit 4 26
スピーチ／自然保護

Unit 5 32
対話文／朝食

Unit 6 38
エッセイ／ジャガイモ

Unit 7 44
エッセイ／漆（うるし）

Unit 8 50
エッセイ／買い物

Unit 9 56
エッセイ／落とし物

Unit 10 62
対話文／マイクロプラスチック

Unit 11 68
エッセイ／キャンプ

Unit 12 74
説明文／フードマイレージ

Unit 13 80
物語／樹医

Unit 14 86
レポート／森林伐採

Unit 15 92
対話文／クイズ

Unit 16 98
スピーチ／フードロス

Unit 17 104
説明文／ドライブ

Unit 18 110
スピーチ／将来の夢

Unit 19 116
説明文／宇宙旅行

Unit 20 122
対話文／ゴミ問題

Unit 21 128
説明文／海の深さを測る

Unit 22 134
説明文／アメリカ先住民

Unit 23 140
エッセイ／日本人と旬

Unit 24 146
スピーチ／OKの起源

Unit 25 152
対話文／待ち合わせ

不規則動詞活用表 158

本書は公立高校入試出題の英文を使用して作成しています（一部改変）。
解説・和訳は著者によるものです。

本書の構成と効果的な使い方

本書では，1つの Unit を6ページで構成しています。

| 英文 | → | 問題 | → | 解答例 | → | 語句リスト | → | ディクテーション | → | 音読 |

① *Let's read!* と ② *Questions*

「読む時間」と「解く時間」を目標に，英文を読んで，問題を解いてみましょう。わからないところがあっても，わかるところから推測して，どんな内容なのかを考えてみましょう。

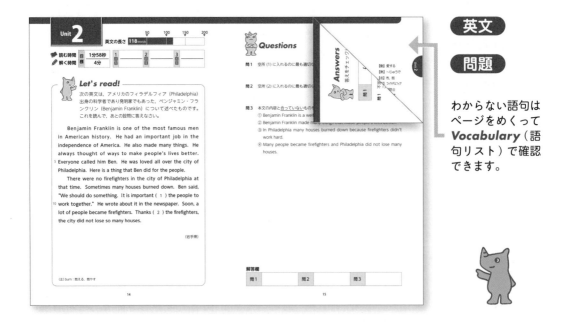

英文

問題

わからない語句はページをめくって *Vocabulary*（語句リスト）で確認できます。

「読む時間」は，高校入試で最初の目標とすべき「1分間に60語」をもとに算出してあります。「解く時間」は，読んだあとに問題を解く時間のめやすです。

③ *Answers*

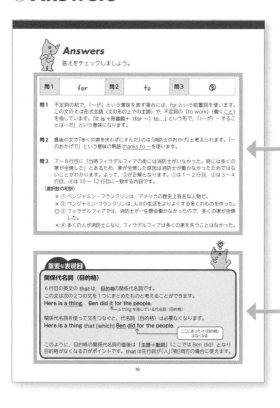

解答例

問題を解き終わったら，必ず答え合わせをして，正解とその理由を確認しましょう。問題を解きっぱなしにしないことが大切です。

問題英文の中から，読むときに「重要な表現」を1つ取り上げて解説しています。

④ *Vocabulary*

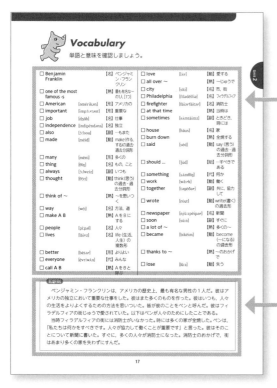

語句リスト

単語の意味を調べるリストとして使うだけでなく，覚えるために活用しましょう。以下，効果的な覚え方をご紹介します。

〈効果があがる！単語の覚え方〉

・単語と意味を声に出して読む。

・意味の欄をシートなどで隠して，単語の意味を言ってみる。

・単語を見て書いたあとに，今度は書いた単語を見ずに，左から右に何度も単語を書いていく。

和訳例

⑤ *Listen & Write!*

　ここは**ディクテーション**のトレーニングコーナーです。ディクテーションとは，音声を聞きながら，聞こえた英文や単語を書き取る勉強法のことです。ただ聞こえたとおりに書き取るだけでなく，次のような「やり方」で効果が何倍にもアップしますよ。

〈効果があがる！ディクテーションのやり方〉

1回目：手にエンピツを持たずに聞いてみる。
　　　　➡ 細かい部分ではなく，文全体の内容を聞き取ってみましょう。

2回目：手にエンピツを持って，聞きながら書き取ってみる。
　　　　➡ 「いつ・どこで・誰が・何を・どうした」を意識して聞きましょう。
　　　　　　書き取るときには，聞こえた音をそのまま書くというよりも，
　　　　　　聞いた内容を自分で英語に直すつもりで書いてみましょう。

　このとき，「複数形の -s」「3単現の -s」「過去形の -ed」など，英語のルールを守っているかどうかを確認しましょう。

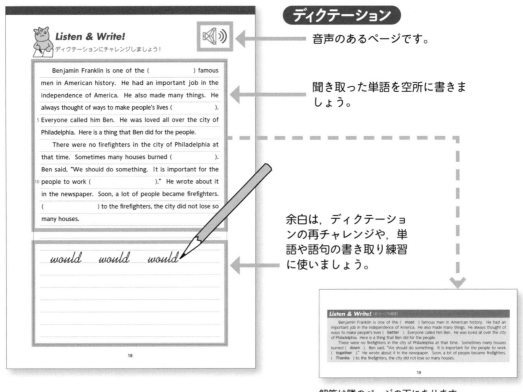

ディクテーション
音声のあるページです。

聞き取った単語を空所に書きましょう。

余白は，ディクテーションの再チャレンジや，単語や語句の書き取り練習に使いましょう。

解答は隣のページの下にあります。

⑥ *Read aloud!*

　ここは**音読**のトレーニングコーナーです。音読とは，文を声に出して読むことです。英語の力がどんどんアップする，効果的な英文の音読の「やり方」をご紹介しましょう。

〈効果があがる！音読のやり方〉

　日本語と英語は語順が違いますね。皆さんは英文を読むとき，意味をとるために後ろから前に戻って「返り読み」をすることがありませんか？　もっと速度を上げて，左から右へとすらすら英文が読めるようにするために，ここではスラッシュで分けられたカタマリごとに，前から意味をとる練習をします。

1回目：スラッシュで分けられたカタマリごとに読まれる英文のあとについて，
　　　　リピートしてみる。
　　　　➡英文の意味を考えながらリピートすることが大切です。
　　　　わからないときは日本語を参考にしましょう。最終的には
　　　　その英文を見ずにリピートできるまで，繰り返し練習しましょう。

2回目：*Listen and Write!* の音声を使い，スラッシュなしの英文を
　　　　何も見ないで聞いてみる。
　　　　➡聞いてそのまま意味がわかるようになるまで，繰り返し聞きましょう。

　ディクテーションや音読は，**英語のままで英語が理解できるようになるためのトレーニング法**です。ディクテーションと音読で，高校入試や大学入試の力をはるかに超えた，本物の英語力を手に入れましょう。最初は難しく感じるかもしれませんが，毎日少しずつ，「明日は必ずできるようになる」という気持ちで**やり続けることが大切**ですよ。

音声について

　本書の *Listen & Write!* と *Read aloud!* の音声は，弊社ホームページで聴くことができます。

https://www.kirihara.co.jp/download/

音声を，ストリーミング（外部サイト）で聴くことができます。ストリーミングをご利用の際には、ご利用の端末がインターネットに接続されている必要があります。

Unit 1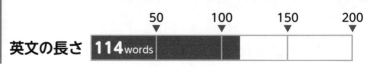

英文の長さ **114**words

| | 50 | 100 | 150 | 200 |

読む時間　目標　**1分54秒**

解く時間　　**2分**

| 1回目 | 2回目 | 3回目 |

Let's read!

次の英文を読み，あとの設問に答えなさい。

　　　Taro became interested in English. He asked his English teacher, Mr. Suzuki, ① (h　　) to study English. Mr. Suzuki said, "The most important thing is to study English every day. You should ② (l　　) to English programs on the radio or watch them 5 on TV at your home. It is also good to read an English newspaper. Many people are now studying English. It is spoken in many countries in the ③ (w　　). We usually use English as a common language when we talk with people ④ (f　　) different countries." After that, he began to study 10 English hard.

　　　Now English is one of his favorite subjects. He is thinking of working in a foreign country in the future.

(愛媛県)

(注) interested：興味を持った　　program：番組　　common：共通の　　favorite：好きな
future：将来

8

Questions

問1 空所①〜④に最も適切な語を1語ずつ入れ，英文を完成させなさい。ただし，それ
ぞれの空所内の文字で始まる語を書くこと。

問2 本文の内容と<u>合っていない</u>ものを選びなさい。
① Mr. Suzuki said it is important to study English every day.
② Mr. Suzuki said we should watch English programs on TV at home.
③ Mr. Suzuki said we should watch news programs on TV at school.
④ Mr. Suzuki said we use English when we talk with people from foreign
countries.

解答欄

問1	①		②		
	③		④		
問2					

Answers

答えをチェックしましょう。

問1	①	how	②	listen
	③	world	④	from
問2	③			

問1　① 英語に興味を持ったタロウがスズキ先生に尋ねた内容なので，「英語の勉強方法」と考えられます。how to ... は「どのように…すべきか，…する方法」となります。

　　　② 空所の後ろに English programs on the radio とあるので，ラジオ番組を「聞く」と考えられます。listen to ～で「～を聞く」となります。

　　　③ 世界共通語の英語がどこで使われるのか，また，多くの国々はどこにあるのかを考えてみましょう。そうすると，「世界」を意味する world を思いつくでしょう。

　　　④ 英語は世界の共通言語として，別の国出身の人々と話すときに使います。「～出身の」という意味を表す場合には，from という前置詞を使います。

問2　5～6行目に「英字新聞を読むこともまたよいことでしょう」とありますが，ニュース番組を見ることは本文で述べられていません。よって，③が正解となります。①は3行目，②は3～5行目，④は7～9行目に一致します。

〈選択肢の和訳〉

　　　× ① スズキ先生は毎日英語を勉強することが大切だと言っていた。

　　　× ② スズキ先生は家ではテレビで英語番組を見るべきだと言っていた。

　　　○ ③ スズキ先生は学校ではテレビでニュース番組を見るべきだと言っていた。

　　　× ④ スズキ先生は私たちが外国から来た人々と話すときには英語を使うと言っていた。

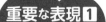

become interested in ～で「～に興味を持つようになる」

be interested in ～「～に興味を持つ」は聞いたことがありますね？　この be（～である）の代わりに become（～になる）を使った表現が，1行目 Taro became interested in English. です。be 動詞と become は，直後に名詞や形容詞などを続けて，同じように使うことができます。I was happy.（私はうれし<u>かった</u>），I became happy.（私はうれしく<u>なった</u>）／ He was a teacher.（彼は教師<u>だった</u>），He became a teacher.（彼は教師に<u>なった</u>）

Vocabulary

単語と意味を確認しましょう。

☐ became	[bikéim]	【動】become (〜になる) の過去形(become - became - become)
☐ English	[íŋgliʃ]	【名】英語 【形】英語の
☐ ask	[ǽsk]	【動】尋ねる
☐ teacher	[tíːtʃər]	【名】先生
☐ how to ...		【熟】…する方法
☐ study	[stʌ́di]	【動】勉強する
☐ said	[séd]	【動】say (言う) の過去・過去分詞形
☐ important	[impɔ́ːrtənt]	【形】重要な
☐ thing	[θíŋ]	【名】こと, もの
☐ every day		【熟】毎日
☐ should ...	[ʃúd]	【助】…すべきである
☐ listen to 〜		【熟】〜を聞く
☐ watch	[wátʃ]	【動】見る
☐ home	[hóum]	【名】家
☐ also	[ɔ́ːlsou]	【副】…もまた
☐ read	[ríːd]	【動】読む
☐ English newspaper		【名】英字新聞
☐ many	[méni]	【形】多くの
☐ people	[píːpəl]	【名】人々
☐ now	[náu]	【副】今では

☐ spoken	[spóukən]	【動】speak (話す) の過去分詞形
☐ country	[kʌ́ntri]	【名】国
☐ in the world		【熟】世界中で
☐ usually	[júːʒuəli]	【副】たいてい, 普通は
☐ use	[júːz]	【動】使う
☐ as 〜	[əz]	【前】〜として
☐ language	[lǽŋgwidʒ]	【名】言葉, 言語
☐ when ...	[hwén]	【接】… (する) ときに
☐ talk with 〜		【熟】〜と話す
☐ different	[dífərənt]	【形】異なった, 別の
☐ after that		【熟】その後
☐ began	[bigǽn]	【動】begin(始める) の過去形
☐ hard	[háːrd]	【副】熱心に
☐ subject	[sʌ́bdʒekt]	【名】学科
☐ think of 〜		【熟】〜について考える, 〜を思いつく
☐ work	[wə́ːrk]	【動】働く
☐ foreign country		【名】外国
☐ in the future		【熟】将来は

和訳例

　タロウは英語に興味を持つようになった。彼は彼の英語の先生のスズキ先生に, どうやって英語を勉強すべきか尋ねた。スズキ先生は言った。「一番大切なことは毎日英語を勉強することです。家で英語番組をラジオで聞いたり, またはテレビで見たりすべきです。英字新聞を読むこともまたよいでしょう。多くの人々が今, 英語を勉強しています。それは世界中の多くの国で話されています。私たちはたいてい, 別の国から来た人々と話すとき英語を共通の言葉として使います」。その後, 彼は英語を熱心に勉強し始めた。

　今では英語は彼の好きな科目の１つである。彼は将来, 外国で働くことを考えている。

Listen & Write!

ディクテーションにチャレンジしましょう！

   Taro became interested in English. He (   )
his English teacher, Mr. Suzuki, how to study English. Mr.
Suzuki said, "The most important thing is to study English
every day. You (   ) listen to English programs
5 on the radio or watch them on TV at your home. It is also
good to read an English newspaper. Many people are now
studying English. It is (   ) in many countries
in the world. We usually use English as a common language
when we talk with people from different countries." After
10 that, he began to study English (   ).
   Now English is one of his favorite (   ).
He is thinking of working in a foreign country in the future.

Read aloud!

音読しましょう！

Taro became interested / in English. / He asked / his English
タロウは興味を持つようになった　　　　英語に　　　　彼は尋ねた　　　彼の英語の先生の

teacher, / Mr. Suzuki, / how to study English. / Mr. Suzuki said, /
スズキ先生に　　　どうやって英語を勉強すべきか　　　　スズキ先生は言った

"The most important thing / is to study English / every day. /
「一番大切なことは　　　　英語を勉強することです　　　　毎日

You should listen / to English programs / on the radio /
あなたは聞くべきです　　　英語番組を　　　　ラジオで

or watch them / on TV / at your home. / It is also good /
またはそれらを見るべきです　テレビで　　家で　　　　またよいでしょう

to read an English newspaper. / Many people / are now studying /
英字新聞を読むことは　　　　多くの人々が　　　今、勉強しています

English. / It is spoken / in many countries / in the world. /
英語を　　それは話されています　　多くの国で　　　世界中の

We usually / use English / as a common language / when we talk /
私たちはたいてい　英語を使います　　共通の言語として　　私たちが話すとき

with people / from different countries." / After that, / he began /
人々と　　　　別の国から来た」　　　　その後　　　彼は始めた

to study English hard. /
英語を熱心に勉強することを

Now / English is / one of his favorite subjects. / He is thinking /
今では　英語は〜である　彼の好きな科目の1つ　　　　彼は考えている

of working / in a foreign country / in the future.
働くことを　　　外国で　　　　将来

Listen & Write! （前ページの解答）

Taro became interested in English. He (**asked**) his English teacher, Mr. Suzuki, how to study English. Mr. Suzuki said, "The most important thing is to study English every day. You (**should**) listen to English programs on the radio or watch them on TV at your home. It is also good to read an English newspaper. Many people are now studying English. It is (**spoken**) in many countries in the world. We usually use English as a common language when we talk with people from different countries." After that, he began to study English (**hard**).

Now English is one of his favorite (**subjects**). He is thinking of working in a foreign country in the future.

13

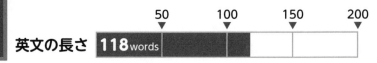

英文の長さ **118** words

読む時間 目標 **1分58秒**
解く時間 **4分**

1回目 _____ 2回目 _____ 3回目 _____

Let's read!

次の英文は，アメリカのフィラデルフィア（Philadelphia）出身の科学者であり発明家でもあった，ベンジャミン・フランクリン（Benjamin Franklin）について述べたものです。これを読んで，あとの設問に答えなさい。

Benjamin Franklin is one of the most famous men in American history. He had an important job in the independence of America. He also made many things. He always thought of ways to make people's lives better.
5 Everyone called him Ben. He was loved all over the city of Philadelphia. Here is a thing that Ben did for the people.

There were no firefighters in the city of Philadelphia at that time. Sometimes many houses burned down. Ben said, "We should do something. It is important (1) the people to
10 work together." He wrote about it in the newspaper. Soon, a lot of people became firefighters. Thanks (2) the firefighters, the city did not lose so many houses.

(岩手県)

(注) burn：燃える，燃やす

Questions

問1　空所 (1) に入れるのに最も適切な前置詞を書きなさい。

問2　空所 (2) に入れるのに最も適切な前置詞を書きなさい。

問3　本文の内容と合っていないものを選びなさい。

① Benjamin Franklin is a well-known person in American history.

② Benjamin Franklin made many things that made people's lives better.

③ In Philadelphia many houses burned down because firefighters didn't work hard.

④ Many people became firefighters and Philadelphia did not lose many houses.

解答欄

問1		問2		問3	

Answers

答えをチェックしましょう。

問1	for	問2	to	問3	③

問1 不定詞の前で、「〜が」という意味を表す場合には、for という前置詞を使います。この文の it は形式主語（文の形の上での主語）で、不定詞の「to work」（働くこと）を指しています。「It is ＋形容詞＋（for 〜）to....」という形で、「（〜が）…することは―だ」という意味になります。

問2 最後の文で「多くの家を失わずにすんだ」のは「消防士のおかげ」と考えられます。「〜のおかげで」という意味の熟語 thanks to 〜を使います。

問3 7〜8行目に「当時フィラデルフィアの街には消防士がいなかった。時には多くの家が全焼した」とあるため、家が全焼した原因は消防士が働かなかったためではないことがわかります。よって、③が正解となります。①は1〜2行目、②は3〜4行目、④は10〜12行目に一致する内容です。

〈選択肢の和訳〉

× ① ベンジャミン・フランクリンは、アメリカの歴史上有名な人物だ。

× ② ベンジャミン・フランクリンは、人々の生活をよりよくする多くのものを作った。

○ ③ フィラデルフィアでは、消防士が一生懸命働かなかったので、多くの家が全焼した。

× ④ 多くの人が消防士になり、フィラデルフィアは多くの家を失うことはなかった。

重要な表現2

関係代名詞（目的格）

6行目の英文の that は、**目的格の関係代名詞**です。

この文は次の2つの文を1つにまとめたものと考えることができます。

Here is a thing.　Ben did it for the people.
　　　　　　　　　　　　a thing を指している代名詞（目的格）

関係代名詞を使って文をつなぐと、代名詞（目的格）は必要なくなります。

Here is a thing that [which] Ben did for the people.

> ここにあった it（目的格）はなくなる

このように、目的格の関係代名詞の直後は「**主語＋動詞**」（ここでは Ben did）となり目的格がなくなるのがポイントです。that は先行詞が「人」「物」両方の場合に使えます。

16

Vocabulary

単語と意味を確認しましょう。

☐ Benjamin Franklin		【名】	ベンジャミン・フランクリン
☐ one of the most famous -s		【熟】	最も有名な〜の1人 [1つ]
☐ American	[əmérikən]	【形】	アメリカの
☐ important	[impɔ́:rtənt]	【形】	重要な
☐ job	[dʒáb]	【名】	仕事
☐ independence	[indipéndəns]	【名】	独立
☐ also	[ɔ́:lsou]	【副】	…もまた
☐ made	[méid]	【動】	make(作る, する)の過去・過去分詞形
☐ many	[méni]	【形】	多くの
☐ thing	[θíŋ]	【名】	もの, こと
☐ always	[ɔ́:lweiz]	【副】	いつも
☐ thought	[θɔ́:t]	【動】	think(思う)の過去・過去分詞形
☐ think of 〜		【熟】	〜を思いつく
☐ way	[wéi]	【名】	方法, 道
☐ make A B		【熟】	AをBにする
☐ people	[pí:pəl]	【名】	人々
☐ lives	[láivz]	【名】	life (生活, 人生) の複数形
☐ better	[bétər]	【形】	よりよい
☐ everyone	[évriwʌ̀n]	【代】	みんな
☐ call A B		【熟】	AをBと呼ぶ

☐ love	[lʌ́v]	【動】	愛する
☐ all over 〜		【熟】	〜じゅうで
☐ city	[síti]	【名】	市, 街
☐ Philadelphia	[filədélfiə]	【名】	フィラデルフィア
☐ firefighter	[fáiərfàitər]	【名】	消防士
☐ at that time		【熟】	当時は
☐ sometimes	[sʌ́mtàimz]	【副】	ときどき, 時には
☐ house	[háus]	【名】	家
☐ burn down		【熟】	全焼する
☐ said	[séd]	【動】	say (言う)の過去・過去分詞形
☐ should …	[ʃúd]	【助】	…すべきである
☐ something	[sʌ́mθìŋ]	【代】	何か
☐ work	[wə́:rk]	【動】	働く
☐ together	[təgéðər]	【副】	共に, 協力して
☐ wrote	[róut]	【動】	write(書く)の過去形
☐ newspaper	[njú:zpèipər]	【名】	新聞
☐ soon	[sú:n]	【副】	すぐに
☐ a lot of 〜		【熟】	多くの〜
☐ became	[bikéim]	【動】	become (〜になる)の過去形
☐ thanks to 〜		【熟】	〜のおかげで
☐ lose	[lú:z]	【動】	失う

Unit 2

和訳例

　ベンジャミン・フランクリンは，アメリカの歴史上，最も有名な男性の１人だ。彼はアメリカの独立において重要な仕事をした。彼はまた多くのものを作った。彼はいつも，人々の生活をよりよくするための方法を思いついた。皆が彼のことをベンと呼んだ。彼はフィラデルフィアの街じゅうで愛されていた。以下はベンが人々のためにしたことである。

　当時フィラデルフィアの街には消防士がいなかった。時には多くの家が全焼した。ベンは，「私たちは何かをすべきです。人々が協力して働くことが重要です」と言った。彼はそのことについて新聞に書いた。すぐに，多くの人々が消防士になった。消防士のおかげで，街はあまり多くの家を失わずにすんだ。

Listen & Write!

ディクテーションにチャレンジしましょう！

Benjamin Franklin is one of the (   ) famous

men in American history. He had an important job in the

independence of America. He also made many things. He

always thought of ways to make people's lives (   ).

5 Everyone called him Ben. He was loved all over the city of

Philadelphia. Here is a thing that Ben did for the people.

There were no firefighters in the city of Philadelphia at

that time. Sometimes many houses burned (   ).

Ben said, "We should do something. It is important for the

10 people to work (   )." He wrote about it

in the newspaper. Soon, a lot of people became firefighters.

(   ) to the firefighters, the city did not lose so

many houses.

Read aloud!

音読しましょう！

Benjamin Franklin / is one of the most famous men /
ベンジャミン・フランクリンは　　　　　　最も有名な男性の1人だ

in American history. / He had an important job / in the independence /
アメリカの歴史上で　　　　　彼は重要な仕事をした　　　　　独立において

of America. / He also made / many things. / He always /
アメリカの　　　　彼はまた作った　　　多くのものを　　　彼はいつも

thought of ways / to make people's lives better. / Everyone called
方法を思いついた　　　人々の生活をよりよくするための　　　皆が彼のことを呼んだ

him / Ben. / He was loved / all over the city / of Philadelphia. / Here is /
ベンと　　彼は愛されていた　　　街じゅうで　　　フィラデルフィアの　　以下〜である

a thing / that Ben did / for the people. /
こと　　　ベンがした　　　人々のために

There were no firefighters / in the city / of Philadelphia /
消防士がいなかった　　　　　　街には　　　　フィラデルフィアの

at that time. / Sometimes / many houses / burned down. / Ben said, /
当時　　　　時には　　　多くの家が　　　全焼した　　　ベンは言った

"We should do / something. / It is important / for the people /
「私たちはすべきです　　何かを　　　　重要です　　　　　人々が

to work together." / He wrote / about it / in the newspaper. / Soon, /
協力して働くことが」　　彼は書いた　そのことについて　　新聞に　　　すぐに

a lot of people / became firefighters. / Thanks to the firefighters, /
多くの人々が　　　　消防士になった　　　　消防士のおかげで

the city did not lose / so many houses.
街は失わずにすんだ　　　あまり多くの家を

Listen & Write! (前ページの解答)

　　Benjamin Franklin is one of the (**most**) famous men in American history. He had an important job in the independence of America. He also made many things. He always thought of ways to make people's lives (**better**). Everyone called him Ben. He was loved all over the city of Philadelphia. Here is a thing that Ben did for the people.

　　There were no firefighters in the city of Philadelphia at that time. Sometimes many houses burned (**down**). Ben said, "We should do something. It is important for the people to work (**together**)." He wrote about it in the newspaper. Soon, a lot of people became firefighters. (**Thanks**) to the firefighters, the city did not lose so many houses.

Unit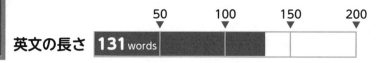

英文の長さ 131 words

50 100 150 200

読む時間 目標 2分11秒
解く時間 4分

1回目 _____
2回目 _____
3回目 _____

 ## Let's read!

次の英文を読み，あとの設問に答えなさい。

We often forget things like names or ideas. Have you ever thought about why we forget those things? Many people have studied about forgetting. Some of them say that there are (1)three types of forgetting.

5　First, we forget things when time passes. For example, the memory of a book you read yesterday is usually stronger than the memory of a book you read last year.

Another type of forgetting happens when we see or read similar things. Think about TV dramas, for example. When
10 you watch two TV dramas and their stories are similar, you will be confused and it will be (　　) to remember details about each TV drama.

Third, (2)we usually forget bad things more quickly than good things. So we have more happy memories of our younger
15 days.

(栃木県)

(注) type(s)：タイプ　　pass：経過する　　memory：記憶，思い出
　　similar：似ている　　drama(s)：ドラマ　　be confused：混乱する　　details：細部

 **Questions**

問1 下線部 (1) の three types（3 つのタイプ）のうち，最初に述べられているのはど
のようなタイプですか。日本語で書きなさい。

Unit 3

問2 空所に入れるのに最も適切な語を，下のア〜エから選びなさい。
ア. wonderful　　イ. important　　ウ. difficult　　エ. interesting

問3 下線部 (2) を書きかえた英文として最も適切なものを選びなさい。
ア. We usually forget good things more quickly than bad things.
イ. We usually forget bad things as quickly as good things.
ウ. We don't forget good things as quickly as bad things.
エ. We don't forget bad things as quickly as good things.

問4 本文に題名をつけるとすると，最も適切なものはどれですか。下のア〜エから選び
なさい。
ア. About things
イ. About forgetting
ウ. Three ways to remember
エ. Memories of our younger days

解答欄

問1	
問2	問3	問4

21

Answers

答えをチェックしましょう。

問1	時間の経過と共に物事を忘れるタイプ				
問2	ウ	問3	ウ	問4	イ

問1　本文で段落が変わるときに出てくる <u>First</u>（最初に，まず）/ <u>Another</u>（もう1つの）/ <u>Third</u>（第3に）という言葉に注目しましょう。これらの後ろに3つのタイプがそれぞれ述べられていることを見抜きましょう。1つ目のタイプは First の直後に述べられています。for example（例えば）の後ろは具体例を示している部分なので解答に加える必要はありません。

問2　本文のテーマは人々が「物事を忘れる」ことです。「忘れる」ということは「思い出すのがどうなることなのか」と考えてみましょう。選択肢の中で意味が合うのは「難しい」という意味の difficult のみです。

〈選択肢の和訳〉

　　×ア．すばらしい　　×イ．重要な　　○ウ．難しい　　×エ．おもしろい

問3　「私たちはたいてい，よいことよりも悪いことをより早く忘れてしまう」が下線部の意味です。よって，ウが正解となります。本文は more … than ～（～よりも…）という比較を使った表現を使っています。一方，ウは not as … as ～（～ほど…ない）という表現を使って，「悪いことほどすぐにはよいことを忘れない」と言いかえています。

〈選択肢の和訳〉

　　×ア．私たちはたいてい，悪いことよりも早くよいことを忘れる。
　　×イ．私たちはたいてい，よいことと同じくらい早く悪いことを忘れる。
　　○ウ．私たちは悪いことほどすぐにはよいことを忘れない。
　　×エ．私たちはよいことほどすぐには悪いことを忘れない。

問4　この文章では，最初の段落で「忘れることの3つのタイプ」というテーマが示されています。そして，それぞれの段落で，その3つのタイプについて述べられています。このテーマと合っている選択肢は「イ」のみです。

〈選択肢の和訳〉

　　×ア．物事について　　　　　　○イ．忘れることについて
　　×ウ．思い出すための3つの方法　×エ．若い頃の思い出

Vocabulary

単語と意味を確認しましょう。

☐ often	[ɔ́:fən]	【副】 しばしば，よく
☐ forget	[fɔrgét]	【動】 忘れる
☐ thing	[θíŋ]	【名】 物事
☐ like ～	[láik]	【前】 ～のような
☐ name	[néim]	【名】 名前
☐ idea	[aidí:ə]	【名】 考え，思いつき
☐ ever	[évər]	【副】〈疑問文で〉これまでに
☐ thought	[θɔ́:t]	【副】 think（思う，考える）の過去・過去分詞形
☐ think about ～		【熟】 ～について考える
☐ why	[hwái]	【副】 どうして
☐ many	[méni]	【形】 多くの
☐ people	[pí:pəl]	【名】 人々
☐ study	[stʌ́di]	【動】 勉強する，研究する
☐ say	[séi]	【動】 言う
☐ first	[fə́:rst]	【副】 最初に，まず
☐ when ...	[hwén]	【接】 …（する）ときに
☐ time	[táim]	【名】 時，時間

☐ for example		【熟】 例えば
☐ read	[réd]	【動】 read（読む）の過去・過去分詞形
☐ usually	[júːʒuəli]	【副】 たいてい
☐ stronger	[strɔ́(:)ŋgər]	【形】 strong（強い）の比較級
☐ another	[ənʌ́ðər]	【形】 もう1つの
☐ happen	[hǽpən]	【動】 起こる
☐ see	[sí:]	【動】 見る
☐ watch	[wátʃ]	【動】 見る
☐ difficult	[dífikʌlt]	【形】 難しい
☐ remember	[rimémbər]	【動】 覚えている，思い出す
☐ each	[í:tʃ]	【形】 それぞれの
☐ third	[θə́:rd]	【副】 第3に
☐ more	[mɔ́:r]	【副】 もっと，より…
☐ quickly	[kwíkli]	【副】 早く，すぐに
☐ so ...	[sóu]	【接】 だから…
☐ younger days		【名】 青春時代，若い頃

Unit 3

和訳例

　私たちは名前や思いつきのような物事をよく忘れる。あなたは私たちがどうしてそのようなことを忘れるのかこれまでに考えたことがあるだろうか。多くの人々が忘れることについて研究してきた。彼らの中のある人々は，忘れることには3つのタイプがあると言っている。

　まず，私たちは時が過ぎると物事を忘れる。例えば，あなたが昨日読んだ本の記憶は，あなたが去年読んだ本の記憶よりもたいてい強い。

　もう1つのタイプの物忘れは，私たちが似たようなものを見たり読んだりするときに生じる。例えば，テレビドラマのことを考えてみよう。あなたが2つのテレビドラマを見て，それらの話が似ているとき，あなたは混乱して，それぞれのテレビドラマについて細かいところを思い出すことは難しいだろう。

　第3に，私たちはたいてい，よいことよりも悪いことをより早く忘れてしまう。そのため，私たちは若い頃のより多くの楽しい記憶を持っているのだ。

Listen & Write!

ディクテーションにチャレンジしましょう！

We often forget things (　　　　　　) names or ideas. Have you ever thought about (　　　　　　) we forget those things? Many people have studied about forgetting. Some of them say that there are three (　　　　　　) of forgetting.

5　　First, we forget things when time passes. For example, the memory of a book you read yesterday is usually stronger than the memory of a book you read last year.

　　Another type of forgetting happens when we see or read (　　　　　　) things. Think about TV dramas, for

10 example. When you watch two TV dramas and their stories are similar, you will be confused and it will be difficult to remember details about each TV drama.

　　Third, we usually forget bad things more (　　　　　　) than good things. So we have more happy memories of our

15 younger days.

Read aloud!
音読しましょう！

We often / forget things / like names or ideas. / Have you ever /
私たちはよく　　物事を忘れる　　　　名前や思いつきのような　　あなたはこれまでにあるだろうか

thought about / why we forget / those things? / Many people /
について考えたことが　　どうして私たちが忘れるのか　　そのようなことを　　多くの人々が

have studied / about forgetting. / Some of them / say that /
研究してきた　　　　忘れることについて　　　　彼らの中のある人々は　　言っている

there are three types / of forgetting. /
３つのタイプがあると　　　　忘れることには

First, / we forget things / when time passes. / For example, /
まず　　　私たちは物事を忘れる　　　時が過ぎると　　　　例えば

the memory / of a book / you read yesterday / is usually stronger /
記憶は　　　本の　　　あなたが昨日読んだ　　　たいてい, より強い

than the memory / of a book / you read / last year. /
記憶よりも　　　　本の　　　あなたが読んだ　　去年

Another type / of forgetting / happens / when we see or read /
もう１つのタイプは　　物忘れの　　　生じる　　私たちが見たり読んだりするときに

similar things. / Think about TV dramas, / for example. /
似たようなものを　　　テレビドラマのことを考えてみよう　　　例えば

When you watch / two TV dramas / and their stories / are similar, /
あなたが見るとき　　２つのテレビドラマを　　そしてそれらの話が　　似ている

you will be confused / and it will be difficult / to remember details /
あなたは混乱するだろう　　　そして難しいだろう　　　細かいところを思い出すことは

about each TV drama. /
それぞれのテレビドラマについて

Third, / we usually forget / bad things / more quickly / than good
第3に　　私たちはたいてい忘れてしまう　　悪いことを　　　より早く　　よいことよりも

things. / So we have / more happy memories / of our younger days.
そのため, 私たちは持っている　　より多くの楽しい記憶を　　　　若い頃の

Listen & Write! (前ページの解答)

We often forget things (　like　) names or ideas. Have you ever thought about (　why　) we forget those things? Many people have studied about forgetting. Some of them say that there are three (　types　) of forgetting.

First, we forget things when time passes. For example, the memory of a book you read yesterday is usually stronger than the memory of a book you read last year.

Another type of forgetting happens when we see or read (　similar　) things. Think about TV dramas, for example. When you watch two TV dramas and their stories are similar, you will be confused and it will be difficult to remember details about each TV drama.

Third, we usually forget bad things more (　quickly　) than good things. So we have more happy memories of our younger days.

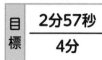

Let's read!

次の文は，ある生徒のスピーチです。これを読んで，あとの設問に答えなさい。

Do you (ア)<u>like</u> climbing mountains?　Some of you will say, "Yes, I do."　Some will say, "No, I don't."　My father (イ)<u>likes</u> climbing mountains.　He has already climbed many famous mountains in Japan.　It was his dream to climb mountains in
5 Nepal.　Last year he visited Nepal to climb them.　He was very happy, 　① 　 his dream came true at last.

　　The mountains there were very beautiful.　Everything looked wonderful, but when he ② <u>(find)</u> a lot of trash like empty cans along the way, he was so 　③ 　.　He wanted to do something to keep
10 nature beautiful.

　　After he came back to Japan, he started to make signs. They said, "Let's keep nature beautiful" in five languages.　He hopes (④) they will be put up in the mountains in Nepal.

　　He often says to me, "The mountains and the rivers are ⑤<u>(cry)</u>.　We
15 have to 　⑥ 　 them.　Everyone should do a good thing for nature now. That's very important."　I (ウ)<u>like</u> his idea.　I'm going to do something to keep nature beautiful (エ)<u>like</u> my father.　Thank you.

(徳島県)

(注) climb：登る　　Nepal：ネパール　　come true：実現する，かなう　　trash：ごみ
empty can：あき缶　　nature：自然　　come back to～：～へ戻ってくる　　sign：立て看板
put up：立てる

Questions

問1 空所①，③，⑥に入れるのに最も適切な語をそれぞれ下のア〜エの中から1つずつ選びなさい。

① ア．if 　　イ．because 　　ウ．but 　　エ．so

③ ア．pretty 　　イ．happy 　　ウ．sad 　　エ．young

⑥ ア．ask 　　イ．say 　　ウ．try 　　エ．save

問2 空所④に入れるのに最も適切な1語を書きなさい。

問3 下線部②，⑤を，それぞれ最も適切な形に直して，1語で書きなさい。

問4 下線部（ア）〜（エ）の like(s) のうち，意味がほかと異なるものを1つ選びなさい。

解答欄

問1	①		③		⑥		問2	
問3	②				⑤		問4	

Answers

答えをチェックしましょう。

問1	①	イ	③	ウ	⑥	エ	問2	that
問3	②	found			⑤	crying		問4	エ

問1　① 空所の前後の関係を考えて選びます。「父親の夢がついにかなった」のが，父親がうれしかった「理由」です。したがって，「なぜなら」という意味で理由を表す，イの because を選びます。so（だから）の場合には，理由を表す文は so の前に置かれます。

〈選択肢の和訳〉

　　　× ア. もし…ならば　○ イ. なぜなら　　× ウ. しかし　　　× エ. だから

　　③ 山中にごみを見つけたときに，山を愛する人がどう感じるのかを考えてみましょう。「悲しい」という意味のウの sad が適切です。

〈選択肢の和訳〉

　　　× ア. かわいい　　× イ. うれしい　　○ ウ. 悲しい　　× エ. 若い

　　⑥ ごみで汚れた自然をどうしなければならないのかを考えてみましょう。「救う」という意味のエの save が適切です。

〈選択肢の和訳〉

　　　× ア. 尋ねる　　　× イ. 言う　　　　× ウ. 試みる　　○ エ. 救う

問2　④の空所には，「that ＋主語＋動詞」という形で「～が…するということ」という意味のカタマリを作る，接続詞の that が入ると考えられます。

問3　② 前後の文の流れから，ここでは過去の出来事について述べているとわかります。find という動詞は find – found – found と不規則変化します。過去形の found に変えましょう。

　　⑤ 文脈からも「泣いている」という意味になると考えられるので，「be 動詞＋動詞の -ing 形」の現在進行形にします。そのために，cry を crying という形に変えます。

問4　like という単語には，動詞として用いて「～を好む」という意味になる場合と，前置詞として用いて「～のように」という意味になる場合とがあります。（ア），（イ），（ウ）の like はすべて「～を好む」という動詞として用いられていますが，（エ）だけは「～のように」という意味の前置詞として用いられています。

Vocabulary

単語と意味を確認しましょう。

☐ like	[láik]	【動】	好む
☐ mountain	[máuntən]	【名】	山
☐ say	[séi]	【動】	言う
☐ already	[ɔ:lrédi]	【副】	〈肯定文で〉すでに
☐ famous	[féiməs]	【形】	有名な
☐ dream	[drí:m]	【名】	夢
☐ visit	[vízət]	【動】	訪れる
☐ because ...	[bikɔ́:z]	【接】	なぜなら…, …なので
☐ at last		【熟】	ついに
☐ when ...	[hwén]	【接】	… (する) ときに
☐ found	[fáund]	【動】	find (見つける) の過去・過去分詞形
☐ a lot of ～		【熟】	多くの～
☐ like ～	[láik]	【前】	～のような
☐ along the way		【熟】	途中で
☐ so	[sóu]	【副】	とても

☐ sad	[sǽd]	【形】	悲しい
☐ want to ...		【熟】	…したいと思う
☐ keep A B		【熟】	AをBに保つ
☐ language	[lǽŋgwidʒ]	【名】	言語, 言葉
☐ hope	[hóup]	【動】	希望する, 願う
☐ often	[ɔ́:fən]	【副】	よく
☐ river	[rívər]	【名】	川
☐ cry	[krái]	【動】	泣く
☐ have to ...		【熟】	…しなければならない
☐ save	[séiv]	【動】	救う
☐ everyone	[évriwʌ̀n]	【代】	みんな
☐ should ...	[ʃúd]	【助】	…すべきである
☐ important	[impɔ́:rtənt]	【形】	重要な
☐ idea	[aidí:ə]	【名】	考え
☐ be going to ...		【熟】	…するつもりだ, …しようとしている

Unit 4

和訳例

　あなたは山に登ることが好きだろうか。あなたがたの何人かは「はい，好きです」と言うだろう。また何人かは「いいえ，好きではないです」と言うだろう。私の父は山に登ることが好きだ。彼はすでに日本の多くの有名な山に登ってきた。ネパールの山々に登ることが彼の夢だった。昨年，彼はその山々に登るためにネパールを訪れた。彼はとても幸せだった，なぜなら，ついに彼の夢がかなったからだ。

　そこの山々はとても美しかった。すべてがすばらしく見えたが，彼が途中であき缶のようなたくさんのごみを見つけたとき，彼はとても悲しかった。彼は自然を美しく保つために何かをしたいと思った。

　彼は日本に帰ってきたあとで，立て看板を作り始めた。それらには５カ国語で，「自然を美しく保とう」と書いてあった。彼はそれらがネパールの山々に立てられることを願っている。

　彼は私によく言う，「山や川は泣いている。私たちはそれらを救わなければならない。今みんなが自然にとってよいことをすべきだ。それがとても重要だ」と。私は彼の考えが好きだ。私は私の父のように自然を美しく保つために何かをするつもりだ。(ご清聴) ありがとうございました。

29

Listen & Write!

ディクテーションにチャレンジしましょう！

Do you like climbing mountains? Some of you will say, "Yes, I do." Some will say, "No, I don't." My father (   ) climbing mountains. He has already climbed many famous mountains in Japan. It was his dream to climb mountains in

5 Nepal. Last year he visited Nepal to climb them. He was very happy, because his dream (   ) (   ) at last.

The mountains there were very beautiful. Everything (   ) wonderful, but when he found a lot

10 of trash like empty cans along the way, he was so sad. He wanted to do something to keep nature beautiful.

After he came back to Japan, he (   ) to make signs. They said, "Let's keep nature beautiful" in five languages. He hopes that they will be (   )

15 (   ) in the mountains in Nepal.

He often says to me, "The mountains and the rivers are crying. We have to save them. Everyone should do a good thing for nature now. That's very important." I like his idea. I'm going to do something to keep nature beautiful like my

20 father. Thank you.

 **Read aloud!**
音読しましょう！

Do you like / climbing mountains? / Some of you / will say, /
あなたは好きだろうか 山に登ることが あなたがたの何人かは 言うだろう

"Yes, I do." / Some will say, / "No, I don't." / My father likes / climbing
「はい，好きです」と また何人かは言うだろう 「いいえ，好きではないです」と 私の父は好きだ 山に登ることが

mountains. / He has already / climbed many famous mountains / in Japan. /
彼はすでに 多くの有名な山に登ってきた 日本の

It was his dream / to climb mountains / in Nepal. / Last year / he visited Nepal /
彼の夢だった 山々に登ることが ネパールの 昨年 彼はネパールを訪れた

to climb them. / He was very happy, / because his dream / came true / at last. /
その山々に登るために 彼はとても幸せだった なぜなら，彼の夢が かなったからだ ついに

The mountains there / were very beautiful. / Everything looked wonderful, /
そこの山々は とても美しかった すべてがすばらしく見えた

but when he found / a lot of trash / like empty cans / along the way, /
だが，彼が見つけたとき たくさんのごみを あき缶のような 途中で

he was so sad. / He wanted / to do something / to keep nature beautiful. /
彼はとても悲しかった 彼は望んだ 何かをすることを 自然を美しく保つために

After he came back / to Japan, / he started / to make signs. / They said, /
彼は帰ってきたあとで 日本に 彼は始めた 立て看板を作ることを それらには書いてあった

"Let's keep nature / beautiful" / in five languages. / He hopes / that they will
「自然を保とう 美しく」 5カ国語で 彼は願っている それらが立てられることを

be put up / in the mountains / in Nepal. /
山々に ネパールの

He often says / to me, / "The mountains / and the rivers / are crying. /
彼はよく言う 私に 「山 そして川は 泣いている

We have to save them. / Everyone should do / a good thing / for nature
私たちはそれらを救わなければならない みんながすべきだ よいことを 自然にとって

now. / That's very important." / I like his idea. / I'm going to do something /
今 それがとても重要だ」 私は彼の考えが好きだ 私は何かをするつもりだ

to keep nature beautiful / like my father. / Thank you.
自然を美しく保つために 私の父のように (ご清聴) ありがとうございました

Listen & Write! (前ページの解答)

Do you like climbing mountains? Some of you will say, "Yes, I do." Some will say, "No, I don't."
My father (**likes**) climbing mountains. He has already climbed many famous mountains in Japan.
It was his dream to climb mountains in Nepal. Last year he visited Nepal to climb them. He was
very happy, because his dream (**came**) (**true**) at last.

The mountains there were very beautiful. Everything (**looked**) wonderful, but when he found
a lot of trash like empty cans along the way, he was so sad. He wanted to do something to keep
nature beautiful.

After he came back to Japan, he (**started**) to make signs. They said, "Let's keep nature
beautiful" in five languages. He hopes that they will be (**put**) (**up**) in the mountains in Nepal.

He often says to me, "The mountains and the rivers are crying. We have to save them.
Everyone should do a good thing for nature now. That's very important." I like his idea. I'm going
to do something to keep nature beautiful like my father. Thank you.

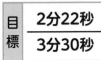 

Unit **5**

英文の長さ **142** words

50 100 150 200

📖 読む時間 | 目標 | **2分22秒**
✏️ 解く時間 | | **3分30秒**

1回目 _____ 2回目 _____ 3回目 _____

Let's read!

次の英文は，ヒル先生（Mr. Hill）とアキ（Aki）の対話です。これを読んで，あとの設問に答えなさい。

Mr. Hill : The first meal of the day is called "breakfast." （ ア ）

Aki : No, I don't.

Mr. Hill : This word has two short words in it: "break" and "fast."

Aki : （ イ ）

5 Mr. Hill : It means "to eat no food." While you are sleeping, you don't eat anything, so you are "fasting." Then, in the morning, you eat the first meal of the day, and "break your fast."

Aki : That's interesting.

10 Mr. Hill : （ ウ ）

Aki : No, I got up late and didn't eat breakfast.

Mr. Hill : （ エ ） Breakfast is the most important meal of the day.

Aki : Really?

15 Mr. Hill : If you don't eat breakfast, you can't have energy for the day.

Aki : I see. （ オ ）

Mr. Hill : You'll feel the difference.

(青森県 改)

(注) meal：食事　fast：断食（する）　energy：活力

32

# Questions

問　空所（ア）～（オ）に入れるのに最も適切な文を，下の1～9の中から1つずつ選
びなさい。

1. I don't know.

2. No, thank you.

3. Oh, didn't you?

4. Do you know why?

5. What does "fast" mean?

6. I don't know what to do.

7. Well, what did you eat for breakfast?

8. Well, did you eat breakfast this morning?

9. I'll get up earlier tomorrow, and eat breakfast.

解答欄

（ア）		（イ）		（ウ）		（エ）		（オ）	

Answers

答えをチェックしましょう。

(ア)	4	(イ)	5	(ウ)	8	(エ)	3	(オ)	9

(ア) アキの No, I don't. という返事につながるように，Yes / No で答える疑問文に絞り込みます。疑問詞で始まる疑問文は，普通 Yes / No では答えません。また，そのあとで，ヒル先生が breakfast という単語を分解していることにも注目しましょう。そうすると，朝食が breakfast と呼ばれる理由を知っているかと尋ねる 4 が正解だとわかります。

(イ) 直後に続く会話で，ヒル先生が fast の意味を説明していることから，アキは fast という単語について質問したのではないかと考え，5 を選びます。

(ウ) 直後で，アキが No と答え，朝食を食べていないことを述べているので，Yes / No で答える疑問文であり，さらに「朝食を食べていない」という内容に自然につながるものを選びます。

(エ) ヒル先生が最も大切なものだと考えている朝食を，アキが食べていなかったことに対する驚きを表す表現が来ると考えられます。didn't you の後ろには eat breakfast が省略されています。これは質問ではなく，アキが朝食を食べていないことへの驚きです。

(オ) ヒル先生から，朝食が大切だというアドバイスを受けたあと，I see.（わかりました）と答えたアキが言うだろうと思われるセリフを選びます。

〈選択肢の和訳〉
1. 知りません。
2. 結構です。
3. おや，そうしなかったのですか。
4. なぜか知っていますか。
5. 「fast」は何を意味するのですか。
6. 私は何をすべきかわかりません。
7. ところで，朝食は何を食べましたか。
8. ところで，今朝は朝食を食べましたか。
9. 明日はもっと早く起きて，朝食を食べます。

重要な表現**3**

Do you know why? は「なぜか知っていますか」

1 行目のヒル先生のセリフの 2 つ目に入る **Do you know why?**（なぜか知っていますか）は，why のあとに the first meal of the day is called "breakfast"（1 日の最初の食事が breakfast と呼ばれるのは）が省略されていると考えられますが，この部分がなくても意味は通じます。このように，「Do you know ＋疑問詞 ?」という形で，いろいろな短い疑問文を作ることができます。例えば，**Do you know when?**（いつなのか知っていますか），**Do you know which?**（どちらなのか知っていますか）などがあります。これらは英語の会話の中でよく使われます。

Vocabulary

単語と意味を確認しましょう。

☐ first	[fə́:rst]	【形】第1の，最初の	
☐ call	[kɔ́:l]	【動】呼ぶ	
☐ know	[nóu]	【動】知っている	
☐ why	[hwái]	【副】なぜ	
☐ word	[wə́:rd]	【名】単語，言葉	
☐ short	[ʃɔ́:rt]	【形】短い	
☐ break	[bréik]	【動】壊す，破る	
☐ mean	[mí:n]	【動】意味する	
☐ eat	[í:t]	【動】食べる	
☐ food	[fú:d]	【名】食べ物	
☐ while ...	[hwáil]	【接】…している間に	
☐ sleep	[slí:p]	【動】眠る（sleep – slept – slept）	

☐ so ...	[sóu]	【接】だから…	
☐ then	[ðén]	【副】それから	
☐ interesting	[íntərəstiŋ]	【形】おもしろい	
☐ well	[wél]	【間】ところで，さて	
☐ get up		【熟】起きる	
☐ late	[léit]	【副】遅く	
☐ important	[impɔ́:rtənt]	【形】重要な	
☐ really	[rí:əli]	【副】本当に	
☐ if ...	[if]	【接】もし…ならば	
☐ see	[sí:]	【動】見る，わかる	
☐ difference	[dífərəns]	【名】違い	

Unit 5

和訳例

Mr. Hill：１日の最初の食事は「breakfast」と呼ばれます。なぜかあなたは知っていますか。

Aki：いいえ，知りません。

Mr. Hill：この言葉は中に２つの短い言葉を持っています。「break」と「fast」です。

Aki：「fast」は何を意味するのですか。

Mr. Hill：それは「to eat no food」（何も食べない）ということを意味します。あなたが寝ている間，あなたは何も食べていません。だから，あなたは「fast」（断食）をしています。その後，朝にその日の最初の食事をして，「break your fast」（あなたの断食を破る）ことになります。

Aki：それはおもしろいですね。

Mr. Hill：さて，今朝あなたは朝食を食べましたか。

Aki：いいえ，私は遅く起きたので朝食を食べませんでした。

Mr. Hill：おや，食べなかったのですか。朝食は１日の中で最も大切な食事なんですよ。

Aki：本当ですか。

Mr. Hill：もしあなたが朝食を食べないと，その日の活力を持つことができません。

Aki：わかりました。私は，明日はもっと早く起きて，朝食を食べます。

Mr. Hill：あなたはその違いを感じるでしょう。

Listen & Write!

ディクテーションにチャレンジしましょう！

Mr. Hill : The first (   ) of the day is called

"breakfast." Do you know why?

Aki : No, I don't.

Mr. Hill : This word has two short words in it: "break" and "fast."

5 Aki : What does "fast" (   )?

Mr. Hill : It means "to eat no food." While you are sleeping,

you don't eat anything, so you are "fasting." Then,

in the morning, you eat the first meal of the day, and

"break your fast."

10 Aki : That's interesting.

Mr. Hill : Well, did you eat breakfast this morning?

Aki : No, I (   ) (   ) late and didn't

eat breakfast.

Mr. Hill : Oh, didn't you? Breakfast is the most important meal

15 of the day.

Aki : Really?

Mr. Hill : If you don't eat breakfast, you can't have energy for

the day.

Aki : I (   ). I'll get up earlier tomorrow and eat

20 breakfast.

Mr. Hill : You'll (   ) the difference.

Read aloud!

音読しましょう！

Mr. Hill: The first meal / of the day / is called / "breakfast." / Do you know / why? /
最初の食事は　　　　1日の　　　呼ばれます　「breakfast」と　あなたは知っていますか　なぜか

Aki: No, / I don't. /
いいえ　知りません

Mr. Hill: This word / has two short words / in it: / "break" and "fast." /
この言葉は　　　2つの短い言葉を持っています　　その中に　　「break」と「fast」です

Aki: What / does "fast" mean? /
何を　　「fast」は意味するのですか

Mr. Hill: It means / "to eat no food." / While you are sleeping, / you don't
それは意味します　「何も食べない」ということを　　　あなたが寝ている間　　　　あなたは何も

eat anything, / so you are "fasting." / Then, / in the morning, /
食べていません　だからあなたは「fast」（断食）をしています　その後　　　朝に

you eat the first meal / of the day, / and "break your fast." /
あなたは最初の食事をします　　　その日の　　そして「あなたの断食を破る」ことになります

Aki: That's interesting. /
それはおもしろいですね

Mr. Hill: Well, / did you eat breakfast / this morning? /
さて　　　あなたは朝食を食べましたか　　　今朝

Aki: No, / I got up late / and didn't eat / breakfast. /
いいえ　私は遅く起きました　だから食べませんでした　朝食を

Mr. Hill: Oh, / didn't you? / Breakfast / is the most important meal / of the day. /
おや　食べなかったのですか　朝食は　　　最も大切な食事なんですよ　　　1日の中で

Aki: Really? /
本当ですか

Mr. Hill: If you don't / eat breakfast, / you can't / have energy / for the day. /
もしあなたがしないなら　朝食を食べる　あなたはできません　活力を持つことが　その日のための

Aki: I see. / I'll get up earlier / tomorrow / and eat breakfast. /
わかりました　私はもっと早く起きます　　明日　　そして朝食を食べます

Mr. Hill: You'll feel the difference.
あなたはその違いを感じるでしょう。

Listen & Write! (前ページの解答)

Mr. Hill : The first (**meal**) of the day is called "breakfast." Do you know why?
Aki : No, I don't.
Mr. Hill : This word has two short words in it: "break" and "fast."
Aki : What does "fast" (**mean**)?
Mr. Hill : It means "to eat no food." While you are sleeping, you don't eat anything, so you are "fasting." Then, in the morning, you eat the first meal of the day, and "break your fast."
Aki : That's interesting.
Mr. Hill : Well, did you eat breakfast this morning?
Aki : No, I (**got**) (**up**) late and didn't eat breakfast.
Mr. Hill : Oh, didn't you? Breakfast is the most important meal of the day.
Aki : Really?
Mr. Hill : If you don't eat breakfast, you can't have energy for the day.
Aki : I (**see**). I'll get up earlier tomorrow and eat breakfast.
Mr. Hill : You'll (**feel**) the difference.

Let's read!

次の英文は，ジュンコが学校での体験学習のあとに書いたものです。これを読んで，あとの設問に答えなさい。

We planted potatoes on the farm near our school today. Our teacher showed us (1) to plant potatoes. First, we put each potato into the ground and (2) put some soil over it. We worked for an hour. It was not easy work but we
5 all felt happy (3) we finished the work. In Hokkaido, we usually plant potatoes in April or May and get new potatoes in August, September or October.

After planting potatoes, our teacher told us some interesting things about potatoes. The first story was about
10 a new kind (4) potato that a man grew on a farm near Hakodate about ninety years ago. Those potatoes were brought from America. The potatoes were easy to grow. They are very popular. They are called "*Danshaku-imo*" (5) the man was a "*Danshaku* (Baron)."

(北海道)

(注) plant：植える　potato(es)：ジャガイモ　ground：地面, 土壌　soil：土
Danshaku：男爵（だんしゃく）。華族の称号の１つで，英語では baron

# Questions

問1　空所 (1) 〜 (5) に入れるのに最も適切な語を選びなさい。

(1) ① which　　② what　　③ how　　④ why

(2) ① yet　　② then　　③ how　　④ when

(3) ① when　　② in　　③ during　　④ with

(4) ① to　　② for　　③ of　　④ in

(5) ① although　　② but　　③ if　　④ because

問2　本文の内容と一致するものを1つ選びなさい。

① ジャガイモを植える作業は簡単だった。

② 北海道では，ジャガイモは植えてから半年以内に収穫できる。

③ 北海道に持ち込まれた新種のジャガイモは，育てるのが難しかった。

④ 北海道に持ち込まれた新種のジャガイモは，貴族専用の高級品であった。

解答欄

		(1)		(2)		(3)	
問1		(4)		(5)			
問2							

Answers

答えをチェックしましょう。

問1	(1)	③	(2)	②	(3)	①
	(4)	③	(5)	④		
問2	②					

問1 (1) show A B は「A（人）に B（物事）を見せる［示す］」という語順で使うことができます。また，空所の次の文ではジャガイモの植え方が記されています。よって，これらから how to ...「…する方法［仕方］」を表す③が最も適切と考えられます。

(2) and の前後の関係に注目すると，出来事が起こった順番で書かれていることがわかります。よって，「それから」と出来事の順番を示す②が最も適切と考えられます。

(3) 空所の直後には「主語＋述語動詞」の形で文が続いているので，前置詞ではなく接続詞が入るのだと考えることができます。選択肢の中で，接続詞は when だけです。前置詞の直後には，文ではなく，名詞や名詞の働きをする語（句）が続きます。

(4) 「a ＋形容詞＋ kind of 〜」という形で，「…な種類の〜」という意味を表します。

(5) 空所の前後には「その男性が『男爵』であった」（原因）→「『ダンシャクイモ』と呼ばれている」（結果）の関係が読み取れます。「A（結果）＋ because ＋ B（原因）」で「B のため A」という意味を表す④が正解です。

問2 選択肢の正解・不正解の理由は以下のようになります。

× ① 4 行目の It was not easy work（それは簡単な作業ではなかった）という部分と矛盾しています。

○ ② 5 〜 7 行目から，半年以内でジャガイモが収穫できるとわかります。

× ③ 12 行目の The potatoes were easy to grow.（そのジャガイモは育てるのが簡単だった）という文と矛盾します。

× ④ 北海道に新種のジャガイモを持ち込んだ人物が「男爵」であったというだけで，貴族専用の高級品だったとはどこにも書いてありません。

重要な表現④

show A B「A（人）に B（物）を示す」と tell A B「A（人）に B（物）を教える［伝える］」

2 行目にある show と 8 行目にある tell という動詞は，それぞれ show A B，tell A B の形で，動詞のあとに「人＋物」の順番で 2 つの名詞を並べて使うことができます。同じ使い方をするものに，give A B「A（人）に B（物）を与える」，lend A B「A（人）に B（物）を貸す」，make A B「A（人）に B（物）を作ってあげる」などがあります。

Vocabulary

単語と意味を確認しましょう。

☐ farm	[fá:rm]	【名】農場
☐ near ～	[níər]	【前】～の近くに [の]
☐ show	[ʃóu]	【動】見せる, 示す
☐ how to ...		【熟】…する方法
☐ first	[fá:rst]	【副】第1には, まず
		【形】最初の
☐ put	[pút]	【動】置く
☐ each	[í:tʃ]	【形】それぞれの
☐ then	[ðén]	【副】それから
☐ over ～	[óuvər]	【前】～の上に
☐ work	[wá:rk]	【動】働く
		【名】仕事, 作業
☐ hour	[áuər]	【名】時間
☐ easy	[í:zi]	【形】簡単な, 楽な
☐ but ...	[bʌt]	【接】しかし…
☐ felt	[félt]	【動】feel (感じる) の過去・過去分詞形
☐ when ...	[hwén]	【接】… (する) ときに
☐ finish	[fíniʃ]	【動】終える
☐ usually	[júːʒuəli]	【副】普通は
☐ April	[éiprəl]	【名】4月

☐ or ...	[ɔ́:r]	【接】または…
☐ May	[méi]	【名】5月
☐ get	[gét]	【動】得る
☐ August	[ɔ́:gəst]	【名】8月
☐ September	[septémbər]	【名】9月
☐ October	[ɑktóubər]	【名】10月
☐ told	[tóuld]	【動】tell (話す) の過去・過去分詞形
☐ interesting	[íntərəstiŋ]	【形】おもしろい
☐ story	[stɔ́:ri]	【名】話
☐ kind	[káind]	【名】種類
☐ grew	[grú:]	【動】grow (育てる) の過去形
☐ ninety	[náinti]	【形】90 の
☐ ～ ago	[əgóu]	【副】～前に
☐ brought	[brɔ́:t]	【動】bring (持ってくる) の過去・過去分詞形
☐ popular	[pɑ́pjələr]	【形】人気のある
☐ call	[kɔ́:l]	【動】呼ぶ
☐ because ...	[bikɔ́:z]	【接】…なので
☐ baron	[bǽrən]	【名】男爵

Unit 6

【和訳例】

　今日，私たちは学校の近くの農場でジャガイモを植えた。先生は私たちにジャガイモの植え方を示してくれた。まず，地面の土の中にそれぞれのジャガイモを置いて，それからその上に土をかけた。私たちは1時間作業をした。それは楽な作業ではなかったが，その作業を終えたときには，私たちはみなうれしく感じた。北海道では，普通4月か5月にジャガイモを植えて8月から9月，10月にかけて新ジャガイモを収穫する。

　ジャガイモを植えたあと，先生が私たちにジャガイモについていくつかおもしろいことを話してくれた。最初の話は，90年ほど前に函館の近くの農場で，ある男性が育てた新種のジャガイモについてだった。それらのジャガイモはアメリカから持ち込まれたものだった。そのジャガイモは育てるのが簡単だった。それらはとても人気がある。その男性が「男爵」だったため，それらは「ダンシャクイモ」と呼ばれている。

Listen & Write!

ディクテーションにチャレンジしましょう！

We planted potatoes on the (   ) near our school today. Our teacher showed us (   ) (   ) plant potatoes. First, we put each potato into the ground and then put some soil over it. We

5 worked for an hour. It was not easy work but we all felt (   ) when we finished the work. In Hokkaido, we usually plant potatoes in April or May and get new potatoes in August, September or October.

After planting potatoes, our teacher told us some

10 interesting things about potatoes. The first story was about a new (   ) of potato that a man grew on a farm near Hakodate about ninety years ago. Those potatoes were brought from America. The potatoes were easy to grow. They are very (   ). They are called *"Danshaku-imo"*

15 because the man was a *"Danshaku* (Baron)."

Read aloud!

音読しましょう！

We planted potatoes / on the farm / near our school / today. /
私たちはジャガイモを植えた　　農場で　　私たちの学校の近くの　　今日

Our teacher / showed us / how to plant potatoes. / First, / we put /
私たちの先生は　私たちに示してくれた　ジャガイモの植え方を　まず　私たちは置いた

each potato / into the ground / and then / put some soil / over it. /
それぞれのジャガイモを　地面の土の中に　それから　土をかけた　その上に

We worked / for an hour. / It was not easy work / but we all felt /
私たちは作業をした　1時間　それは楽な作業ではなかった　だが私たちはみなうれしく感じた

happy / when we finished / the work. / In Hokkaido, / we usually /
うれしく　私たちが終えたときには　その作業を　北海道では　私たちは普通

plant potatoes / in April / or May / and get new potatoes in August, /
ジャガイモを植える　4月に　または5月に　そして8月に新ジャガイモを収穫する

September / or October. /
9月に　または10月に

After planting potatoes, / our teacher told us / some interesting
ジャガイモを植えたあと　先生が私たちに話してくれた　いくつかおもしろいことを

things / about potatoes. / The first story / was about /
ジャガイモについて　最初の話は　についてだった

a new kind of potato / that a man grew / on a farm / near Hakodate /
新種のジャガイモ　ある男性が育てた　農場で　函館の近くの

about ninety years ago. / Those potatoes / were brought /
90年ほど前に　それらのジャガイモは　持ち込まれた

from America. / The potatoes / were easy / to grow. /
アメリカから　そのジャガイモは　簡単だった　育てるのが

They are very popular. / They are called / *"Danshaku-imo"* /
それらはとても人気がある　それらは呼ばれている　「ダンシャクイモ」と

because the man / was a *"Danshaku* (Baron)."
なぜならその男性が　「男爵」だったため

Listen & Write! (前ページの解答)

We planted potatoes on the (**farm**) near our school today. Our teacher showed us (**how**) (**to**) plant potatoes. First, we put each potato into the ground and then put some soil over it. We worked for an hour. It was not easy work but we all felt (**happy**) when we finished the work. In Hokkaido, we usually plant potatoes in April or May and get new potatoes in August, September or October.

After planting potatoes, our teacher told us some interesting things about potatoes. The first story was about a new (**kind**) of potato that a man grew on a farm near Hakodate about ninety years ago. Those potatoes were brought from America. The potatoes were easy to grow. They are very (**popular**). They are called *"Danshaku-imo"* because the man was a *"Danshaku* (Baron)."

Unit 7

英文の長さ **156** words

📖 読む時間 目標 **2分36秒**
✏️ 解く時間 標 **4分30秒**

1回目	2回目	3回目
———	———	———

Let's read!

次の英文を読み，あとの設問に答えなさい。

　Urushi has been used in many different ways. *Urushi* can also be used for restoring crafts. (　1　) *Urushi* is used for small crafts, and also for buildings made of wood. It was also used to build Kinkakuji Temple in Kyoto. Of course, a lot of *urushi*
5 is needed for restoring buildings. (　2　) Many old buildings in World Heritage Sites in Nikko also need a lot of *urushi*. (　3　) In fact, the number of Japanese workers who produce *urushi* is decreasing. These days, Japan is trying to produce all of the *urushi* needed to restore important traditional buildings like
10 these only in Japan.

(埼玉県 改)

(注) restore：修復する　　craft：工芸品

44

Questions

問　空所 (1) ～ (3) に入れるのに最も適切な文を下のア～カの中から 1 つずつ選びなさい。

ア．However, almost all of the *urushi* used in Japan comes from abroad, and only 3% of the *urushi* used in Japan is made in the country.

イ．However, most of them don't need to be painted with *urushi* made in Japan because *urushi* made in other countries is better.

ウ．For example, about 1,500 kg of *urushi* was used to restore Kinkakuji Temple.

エ．For example, if you break a dish, you can restore it by using *urushi* as a bonding agent.

オ．But Kinkakuji Temple in Kyoto has been preserved for a long time.

カ．It is because *urushi* made in Japan is too expensive to use for restoring.

解答欄

(1)		(2)		(3)	

Answers

答えをチェックしましょう。

(1)	エ	(2)	ウ	(3)	ア

(1) 直前の文に「漆はまた工芸品の修復にも使用可能だ」とあるため，空所には漆を使って工芸品を修復する例が入ると考えられます。よって，エが最も適切だとわかります。説明のあとで具体的な例を示し，読み手がよりよく内容を理解できるように書かれています。この英文の流れを覚えておきましょう。

(2) 空所の前に「漆はまた，京都の金閣寺を建築するためにも使われた。もちろん，建物を修復するためには大量の漆が必要とされる」とあるため，空所にはどのくらい大量の漆が必要とされるかの例が入ると考えられます。よって，ウが最も適切だとわかります。

(3) 空所前までは，漆のさまざまな用途や，建物を修復するときに大量の漆が必要であることが書かれています。一方，空所後には，漆を生産する日本人労働者の数は減りつつあり，必要な漆を日本だけで生産する努力をしていることが書かれています。この前後の関係をつなぐには，「大量に漆が必要だが，日本で生産される漆の量は少ない」というような内容の文が入るとよいと考えられます。よって，アが最も適切だとわかります。

〈選択肢の和訳〉

ア．しかし，日本で使われるほぼすべての漆は外国から来ており，日本で使われる漆のわずか３％だけが国内で作られている。

イ．しかし，それらのほとんどは，他国で作られた漆のほうがよいので，日本で作られた漆で塗る必要はない。

ウ．例えば，金閣寺を修復するには約 1,500kg の漆が使われた。

エ．例えば，皿を割ったならば，漆を接着剤として使うことで皿を修復することができる。

オ．しかし，京都の金閣寺は長い間保存されてきた。

カ．それは，日本で作られる漆があまりに高価すぎて修復に使えないからだ。

重要な表現 5

be 動詞＋-ing の 2 つの意味

通常，「be動詞＋-ing」は，He is playing the piano.（彼はピアノをひいているところだ）のように，「…しているところだ」（＝行為中の動作）の意味で用いられます。しかし，本文の最後の2文にある，… is decreasing（減りつつある），… is trying to produce（生産しようと努力しつつある）」は「…しつつある」（＝ある方向に向かっている）の意味で用いられています。同じ形でも意味が違う場合があるので注意しましょう。

Vocabulary

単語と意味を確認しましょう。

☐ have[has] been used		【熟】	ずっと使われてきた
☐ in many different ways		【熟】	さまざまな方法で
☐ also	[ɔ́:lsou]	【副】	また
☐ for example		【熟】	例えば
☐ break	[bréik]	【動】	壊す，割る
☐ dish	[díʃ]	【名】	皿
☐ bonding agent		【名】	接着剤
☐ building	[bíldiŋ]	【名】	建物
☐ made of ～		【熟】	～で作られた，～製の
☐ wood	[wúd]	【名】	木材
☐ build	[bíld]	【動】	建築する
☐ temple	[témpəl]	【名】	寺
☐ of course		【熟】	もちろん
☐ a lot of ～		【熟】	大量の～，数多くの～
☐ need	[ní:d]	【動】	必要とする
☐ World Heritage Site		【名】	世界遺産
☐ however	[hauévər]	【副】	しかし
☐ almost all of ～		【熟】	ほぼすべての～
☐ come from ～		【熟】	～から来る
☐ abroad	[əbrɔ́:d]	【副】	外国で
☐ in fact		【熟】	実際に
☐ the number of ～		【熟】	～の数
☐ produce	[prədjú:s]	【動】	生産する
☐ decrease	[dì:krí:s]	【動】	減少する
☐ these days		【熟】	最近，近頃では
☐ try to ...		【熟】	... しようと努力する
☐ important	[impɔ́:rtənt]	【形】	重要な
☐ traditional	[trədíʃənəl]	【形】	伝統的な
☐ like	[láik]	【前】	～のような

Unit 7

和訳例

　漆はさまざまな方法でずっと使われてきた。漆はまた工芸品の修復にも使用可能だ。例えば，皿を割ったならば，漆を接着剤として使うことで皿を修復することができる。漆は小さな工芸品や，木造の建物にも使われる。漆はまた，京都の金閣寺を建築するためにも使われた。もちろん，建物を修復するためには大量の漆が必要とされる。例えば，金閣寺を修復するには約1,500kgの漆が使われた。日光にある世界遺産の多くの古い建物もまた，大量の漆を必要としている。しかし，日本で使われるほぼすべての漆は外国から来ており，日本で使われる漆のわずか3％だけが国内で作られている。実際，漆を生産する日本人労働者の数は減りつつある。最近，日本はこうした重要な伝統的建造物を修復するために必要な漆をすべて日本だけで生産しようとしている。

47

Listen & Write!

ディクテーションにチャレンジしましょう！

Urushi has been used in (   ) different ways. *Urushi* can also be used for restoring crafts. For example, if you (   ) a dish, you can restore it by using *urushi* as a bonding agent. *Urushi* is used for small crafts, and

5 also for buildings made of wood. It was also used to build Kinkakuji Temple in Kyoto. Of course, a lot of *urushi* is needed for restoring buildings. For example, about (   ) kg of *urushi* was used to restore Kinkakuji Temple. Many old buildings in World Heritage Sites in Nikko also need a lot

10 of *urushi*. (   ), almost all of the *urushi* used in Japan comes from abroad, and only 3% of the *urushi* used in Japan is made in the country. In fact, the number of Japanese (   ) who produce *urushi* is decreasing. These days, Japan is trying to produce all of the *urushi* needed to

15 restore important traditional buildings like these only in Japan.

Read aloud!
音読しましょう！

Urushi has been used / in many different ways. / *Urushi* can also
漆はずっと使われてきた　　　　　さまざまな方法で　　　　　　　漆はまた使用可能だ

be used / for restoring crafts. / For example, / if you break a dish, /
　　　　工芸品を修復するのに　　　　例えば　　　　皿を割ったならば

you can restore it / by using *urushi* / as a bonding agent. / *Urushi* is used /
それを修復することができる　漆を使うことによって　　接着剤として　　　漆は使われる

for small crafts, / and also for buildings / made of wood. / It was also
小さな工芸品に　　　　そして建物にも　　　　木材で作られた　　それはまた使われた

used / to build Kinkakuji Temple / in Kyoto. / Of course, / a lot of *urushi*
　　金閣寺を建築するために　　　京都の　　もちろん　　大量の漆が必要とされる

is needed / for restoring buildings. / For example, / about 1,500 kg of
　　　　建物を修復するためには　　　　例えば　　　約1,500kgの漆が使われた

urushi was used / to restore Kinkakuji Temple. / Many old buildings /
　　　　　　　　金閣寺を修復するために　　　　多くの古い建物は

in World Heritage Sites / in Nikko / also need a lot of *urushi*. / However, /
世界遺産の　　　　　　日光にある　　また大量の漆を必要としている　　しかし

almost all of the *urushi* / used in Japan / comes from abroad, /
ほぼすべての漆は　　　　日本で使われる　　　外国から来る

and only 3% of the *urushi* / used in Japan / is made / in the country. /
漆のわずか3％だけが　　　　日本で使われる　　作られている　　その国［日本］で

In fact, / the number of Japanese workers / who produce *urushi* /
実際　　　日本人労働者の数は　　　　　　漆を生産する

is decreasing. / These days, / Japan is trying to produce / all of the *urushi* /
減りつつある　　　最近　　日本は生産しようとしている　　漆のすべてを

needed to restore / important traditional buildings / like these / only in
修復するために必要な　　　重要な伝統的建造物を　　　こうした　　日本だけで

Japan.

Listen & Write! （前ページの解答）

    Urushi has been used in (**many**) different ways. *Urushi* can also be used for restoring crafts. For example, if you (**break**) a dish, you can restore it by using *urushi* as a bonding agent. *Urushi* is used for small crafts, and also for buildings made of wood. It was also used to build Kinkakuji Temple in Kyoto. Of course, a lot of *urushi* is needed for restoring buildings. For example, about (**1,500**) kg of *urushi* was used to restore Kinkakuji Temple. Many old buildings in World Heritage Sites in Nikko also need a lot of *urushi*. (**However**), almost all of the *urushi* used in Japan comes from abroad, and only 3% of the *urushi* used in Japan is made in the country. In fact, the number of Japanese (**workers**) who produce *urushi* is decreasing. These days, Japan is trying to produce all of the *urushi* needed to restore important traditional buildings like these only in Japan.

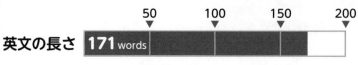

Unit **8**

英文の長さ **171** words

| | 50 | 100 | 150 | 200 |

📖 読む時間
✏️ 解く時間

目標

2分51秒
4分

1回目 —————
2回目 —————
3回目 —————

Let's read!

次の英文を読み，あとの設問に答えなさい。

I have a lot of work to do every day. I don't have much time to go shopping. I usually go to a supermarket, because I can get many kinds of food in one place.

A supermarket is large but there are not so many people
5 who work in it, and <u>they don't have time to talk to me</u> because they have a lot to do and I don't want to bother them.

I sometimes go to a small shop which sells meat, fish or fruit. I can't finish all my shopping in one place, but it has something good that a supermarket doesn't have. People
10 working in a small shop often talk to me, and I can talk about a lot of things with them when I buy food.

In that way, a supermarket is a good place for shopping in my (1) life. On the other hand, a small food shop is not only a place for shopping. It is also a good place for me to (2).

(大分県)

(注) bother：困らせる

50

# Questions

問1　本文の内容から考えて、下線部のように言える理由は何ですか。日本語で書きなさい。

問2　空所 (1) に入れるのに最も適切な語を下のア〜エから 1 つ選びなさい。
　　ア．early　　　イ．busy　　　ウ．long　　　エ．happy

問3　空所 (2) に入れるのに最も適切なものを下のア〜エから 1 つ選びなさい。
　　ア．enjoy talking　　　　　イ．find good food
　　ウ．do a lot of work　　　エ．get any food I want

Unit 8

解答欄

問1	
問2	問3

Answers

答えをチェックしましょう。

問1	従業員にはやるべきことがたくさんあるので。		
問2	イ	問3	ア

問1　下線部の直後には because（…なので）という理由を述べる接続詞があるので，because 以下に下線部の理由が述べられています。この設問のように理由を書く場合は，「…なので，…から」と答えるように注意しましょう。

問2　筆者の意見をまとめると，次のようになります。
　　　スーパーマーケット
　　　　（利点）１カ所で多くの種類の食べ物が買える。
　　　　（欠点）話をすることができない。
　　　小さな商店
　　　　（利点）話をすることができる。
　　　　（欠点）１つの店舗だけでは買い物を終えることができない。
　　　　このことから考えて，スーパーマーケットは busy life（忙しい生活）において便利な場所だと考えることができます。
　　　〈選択肢の和訳〉
　　　　×ア．早い　　　〇イ．忙しい　　　×ウ．長い　　　×エ．幸福な

問3　問2の解説で示した利点と欠点から，小さな店の利点は「話ができること」です。そのことを表すアの enjoy talking（話を楽しむ）を選びます。
　　　〈選択肢の和訳〉
　　　　〇ア．話を楽しむ　　　×イ．よい食べ物を見つける
　　　　×ウ．多くの仕事をする　　×エ．私がほしいどんな食べ物でも手に入れる

重要な表現⑥

「…して楽しむ」は enjoy -ing

問3の選択肢にあるように，enjoy「楽しむ」という動詞のあとに「…することを」という意味を続ける場合は，動詞に -ing が付いた**動名詞**を置きます。普通，「…することを」の意味で動詞を続ける場合は，I like playing tennis. ＝ I like to play tennis. の like のように，動名詞でも不定詞でも同じように使えますが，以下のように動名詞か不定詞のどちらかしか使えない動詞もあるので注意が必要です。

enjoy -ing（…して楽しむ）　　　decide to ...（…することに決める）
finish -ing（…し終える）　　　hope to ...（…することを望む）

52

Vocabulary

単語と意味を確認しましょう。

□ a lot of ~		【熟】	多くの~
□ work	[wə́ːrk]	【名】	仕事, 作業
		【動】	働く
□ every day		【熟】	毎日
□ go shopping		【熟】	買い物に行く
□ usually	[júːʒuəli]	【副】	普通は
□ supermarket	[súːpərmàːrkət]	【名】	スーパーマーケット
□ because ...	[bikɔ́ːz]	【接】	…なので
□ can ...	[kən]	【助】	…できる
□ get	[gét]	【動】	得る
□ many	[méni]	【形】	多くの
□ kind	[káind]	【名】	種類
□ food	[fúːd]	【名】	食べ物
□ place	[pléis]	【名】	場所
□ large	[láːrdʒ]	【形】	広い
□ but ...	[bʌ́t]	【接】	しかし…
□ so	[sóu]	【副】	〈否定文で〉それほど
□ people	[píːpəl]	【名】	人々
□ talk to ~		【熟】	~と話す
□ want to ...		【熟】	…したいと思う
□ sometimes	[sʌ́mtàimz]	【副】	ときどき
□ small	[smɔ́ːl]	【形】	小さい
□ shop	[ʃáp]	【名】	店
□ sell	[sél]	【動】	売る
□ meat	[míːt]	【名】	肉
□ fish	[fíʃ]	【名】	魚
□ fruit	[frúːt]	【名】	果物
□ finish	[fíniʃ]	【動】	終える
□ often	[ɔ́ːfən]	【副】	よく, しばしば
□ talk about ~		【熟】	~について話す
□ when ...	[hwén]	【接】	…（する）ときに
□ buy	[bái]	【動】	買う
□ in that way		【熟】	そのように
□ busy	[bízi]	【形】	忙しい
□ life	[láif]	【名】	生活
□ on the other hand		【熟】	一方で
□ only	[óunli]	【副】	ただ…だけ
□ also	[ɔ́ːlsou]	【副】	…もまた
□ enjoy -ing		【熟】	…することを楽しむ

Unit 8

【和訳例】

　私は毎日やるべきたくさんの仕事を持っている。私は買い物に行くための時間をあまり多く持っていない。私はたいてい，スーパーマーケットに行く，なぜなら１つの場所でたくさんの種類の食べ物を買うことができるからだ。

　スーパーマーケットは広いが，そこで働いている人はあまり多くいない，そして彼らにはやるべきことがたくさんあるので従業員は私と話す時間はないし，私は彼らを困らせたくない。

　私はときどき，肉や魚や果物を売る小さな商店に行く。私は１つの場所で自分の買い物を全部すませることはできないが，そのお店はスーパーマーケットが持っていない何かよいものを持っている。小さな商店で働いている人々はよく私に話しかけてくれるし，私は食べ物を買うとき彼らといろいろなことについて話すことができる。

　そのように，スーパーマーケットは私の忙しい生活の中での買い物のためにはよい場所である。その一方で，小さな食料品店は買い物のための場所というだけではない。そこはまた，私にとって会話を楽しむためのよい場所でもある。

Listen & Write!
ディクテーションにチャレンジしましょう！

I have a lot of work to do every day. I don't have much time to go (   ). I usually go to a supermarket, because I can get many kinds of food in one place.

5   A supermarket is large but there are not so many people who work in it, and they don't (   ) time to talk to me because they have a lot to do and I don't want to bother them.

I sometimes go to a small shop which sells meat, fish or 10 fruit. I can't (   ) all my shopping in one place, but it has something good that a supermarket doesn't have. People working in a small shop often talk to me, and I can talk about a lot of things with them when I buy food.

In that way, a supermarket is a good place for shopping in 15 my busy life. On the other (   ), a small food shop is not (   ) a place for shopping. It is also a good place for me to enjoy talking.

Read aloud!

音読しましょう！

I have / a lot of work / to do / every day. / I don't have /
私は持っている　　　たくさんの仕事を　　　やるべき　　　毎日　　　私は持っていない

much time / to go shopping. / I usually go / to a supermarket, /
あまり多くの時間を　　　買い物に行くための　　　私はたいてい行く　　　スーパーマーケットに

because I can get / many kinds of food / in one place. /
なぜなら私は買うことができるからだ　　　たくさんの種類の食べ物を　　　1つの場所で

A supermarket / is large / but there are not / so many people /
スーパーマーケットは　　　広い　　　しかしいない　　　あまり多くの人が

who work in it, / and they don't have time / to talk to me / because
その中で働いている　　　そして彼らには時間がない　　　私と話すための　　　なぜなら

they have a lot to do / and I don't want to bother them. /
彼らにはやるべきことがたくさんあるので　　　そして私は彼らを困らせたくない

I sometimes / go to a small shop / which sells meat, fish or fruit. /
私はときどき　　　小さな商店に行く　　　肉や魚、果物を売る

I can't finish all my shopping / in one place, / but it has /
私は自分の買い物を全部すませることはできない　　　1つの場所で　　　しかしそれは持っている

something good / that a supermarket / doesn't have. / People /
何かよいものを　　　スーパーマーケットが　　　持っていない　　　人々は

working in a small shop / often talk to me, / and I can talk /
小さな商店で働いている　　　よく私に話しかけてくれる　　　そして私は話すことができる

about a lot of things / with them / when I buy food. /
いろいろなことについて　　　彼らと　　　私が食べ物を買うとき

In that way, / a supermarket / is a good place / for shopping /
そのように　　　スーパーマーケットは　　　よい場所である　　　買い物のためには

in my busy life. / On the other hand, / a small food shop /
私の忙しい生活の中で　　　その一方で　　　小さな食料品店は

is not only a place / for shopping. / It is also / a good place / for me /
場所というだけではない　　　買い物のための　　　そこはまた　　　よい場所でもある　　　私にとって

to enjoy talking.
会話を楽しむための

Unit 8

Listen & Write! (前ページの解答)

　　I have a lot of work to do every day. I don't have much time to go (**shopping**). I usually go to a supermarket, because I can get many kinds of food in one place.

　　A supermarket is large but there are not so many people who work in it, and they don't (**have**) time to talk to me because they have a lot to do and I don't want to bother them.

　　I sometimes go to a small shop which sells meat, fish or fruit. I can't (**finish**) all my shopping in one place, but it has something good that a supermarket doesn't have. People working in a small shop often talk to me, and I can talk about a lot of things with them when I buy food.

　　In that way, a supermarket is a good place for shopping in my busy life. On the other (**hand**), a small food shop is not (**only**) a place for shopping. It is also a good place for me to enjoy talking.

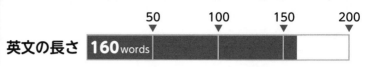

読む時間　目標　2分40秒
解く時間　　　　5分

1回目 ──── 2回目 ──── 3回目 ────

Let's read!

次の英文は，英語の授業で読んだ英字新聞の記事の一部です。これを読んで，あとの設問に答えなさい。

I heard a story from one of (1). It happened to her a month ago. When she was going to buy a train ticket at a station, her wallet was not in her bag. She looked for it (2) but couldn't find it. She didn't know (3). Suddenly a young

5 man spoke to her. He spoke a foreign language she didn't know. She said, "No! No!" and tried to walk (4). But he followed her, and she was surprised. When she tried to run away from him, he touched her arm. She was afraid and looked at him. He smiled, showed her a wallet, and (5).

10 Then she understood everything. "Oh, I dropped it. He found it and wanted to give it back to me," she thought. She didn't know what language he spoke, but she said to him, "Thank you very much." He smiled again and walked away.

(東京都)

(注) wallet：財布　　drop：落とす

56

Questions

問1 空所 (1) 〜 (5) に入れるのに最も適切なものを下のア〜エの中から 1 つずつ選びなさい。

(1) ア．Japanese my friend　　イ．my Japanese friends
　　ウ．my Japanese friend　　エ．Japanese my friends

(2) ア．for a while　　イ．as a while
　　ウ．for while　　エ．as while

(3) ア．what doing　　イ．what to doing
　　ウ．to what do　　エ．what to do

(4) ア．from away him　　イ．away from him
　　ウ．from he away　　エ．away from he

(5) ア．gave her to it　　イ．gave it her
　　ウ．gave it to her　　エ．gave it to she

問2 本文の内容と合っているものを 1 つ選びなさい。

ア．The woman looked for her bag at the station but didn't find it.

イ．The young man smiled and said to the woman, "Thank you very much."

ウ．The young man followed the woman because he wanted to give her the wallet.

エ．The woman spoke to the young man in Japanese because she didn't know what to do.

解答欄

問1	(1)		(2)		(3)		(4)		(5)	
問2										

Answers

答えをチェックしましょう。

問1	(1)	イ	(2)	ア	(3)	エ	(4)	イ	(5)	ウ
問2	ウ									

問1 （1）my のような所有格の代名詞や，冠詞の a や the は，その他のさまざまな形容詞よりも前に置かれます。また，<u>one of ～</u>（～の1人）という表現は，「(複数の人がいるうち) の1人」という意味なので，～の部分には<u>複数形の名詞</u>が置かれます。

（2）<u>while</u> は「しばらくの間」という意味の名詞としても使うことができますが，その場合は，<u>a</u> という冠詞が付きます。また，「～の間」という期間を表す前置詞は <u>for</u> です。for a while (しばらくの間) という熟語として覚えておきましょう。

（3）「**疑問詞＋不定詞**」は名詞の働きをします。what to ... だと，「何を…するのか」という意味になります。同様の表現では，how to ...（どのように…するのか）が重要です。

（4）<u>away from ～</u>は，「～から離れて」という意味の，2語で1つの前置詞の働きをする熟語です。また，前置詞のあとに代名詞を置く場合は，目的格（ここでは him）が続くことにも注意しましょう。

（5）give という動詞は直後の語順が大切です。「**give ＋人＋物**」と「**give ＋物＋to ＋人**」という2つの語順があることを知っておきましょう。動詞の目的語に代名詞を置く場合は，her のような目的格が使われることにも注意しましょう。

問2 選択肢の正解・不正解の理由は以下のようになります。
ア．女性が探していたのは財布 (wallet) で，かばん (bag) ではありません。
イ．「どうもありがとう」と言ったのは男性ではなく，女性のほうです。
ウ．本文後半の内容と一致しています。
エ．女性が男性に日本語で話している場面はありません。また，最後に Thank you very much. と英語で話しています。

〈選択肢の和訳〉
×ア．女性は駅で彼女のかばんを探したが，それは見つからなかった。
×イ．若い男性はほほ笑んで女性に「どうもありがとう」と言った。
○ウ．若い男性は，女性に財布を渡したかったので，女性のあとについてきた。
×エ．女性はどうしていいかわからなかったので，若い男性に日本語で話しかけた。

Vocabulary

単語と意味を確認しましょう。

☐ heard	[hə́:rd]	【動】hear (聞く) の過去・過去分詞形
☐ story	[stɔ́:ri]	【名】話, 物語
☐ Japanese friend		【名】日本人の友達
☐ happen to ～		【熟】～に起こる
☐ month	[mʌ́nθ]	【名】月, ひと月
☐ ～ ago	[əgóu]	【副】～前に
☐ when ...	[hwén]	【接】…(する) ときに
☐ be going to ...		【熟】…しようとしている, …するつもりだ
☐ buy	[bái]	【動】買う
☐ train ticket		【名】電車の切符
☐ station	[stéiʃən]	【名】駅
☐ look for ～		【熟】～を探す
☐ for a while		【熟】しばらくの間
☐ but ...	[bʌ́t]	【接】しかし…
☐ find	[fáind]	【動】見つける
☐ know	[nóu]	【動】知っている, わかる
☐ what to ...		【熟】何を…すべきか
☐ suddenly	[sʌ́dənli]	【副】突然
☐ spoke	[spóuk]	【動】speak (話す) の過去形
☐ speak to ～		【熟】～に話しかける
☐ foreign language		【名】外国語
☐ try to ...		【熟】…しようと試みる
☐ walk away from ～		【熟】～から歩き去る
☐ follow	[fálou]	【動】ついてくる
☐ surprised	[sərpráizd]	【形】驚いて
☐ run away from ～		【熟】～から走って逃げる
☐ touch	[tʌ́tʃ]	【動】触れる, 触る
☐ arm	[á:rm]	【名】腕
☐ afraid	[əfréid]	【形】恐れて, 怖がって
☐ look at ～		【熟】～を見る
☐ smile	[smáil]	【動】ほほ笑む
☐ show A B		【熟】A に B を見せる
☐ gave	[géiv]	【動】give (与える, 手渡す) の過去形
☐ then	[ðén]	【副】そのとき, それで
☐ understood	[ʌ̀ndərstúd]	【動】understand (理解する) の過去・過去分詞形
☐ everything	[évriθiŋ]	【代】すべてのこと
☐ want to ...		【熟】…したいと思う
☐ give back to ～		【熟】～へ返す
☐ thought	[θɔ́:t]	【動】think (思う, 考える) の過去・過去分詞形
☐ again	[əgén]	【副】もう一度, また

Unit 9

和訳例

　私は日本人の友達の1人からある話を聞いた。それは1カ月前に彼女に起こった。彼女が駅で電車の切符を買おうとしたとき, 彼女の財布がかばんの中になかった。彼女はしばらくそれを探したが, 見つけることができなかった。彼女はどうしたらよいのかわからなかった。突然, 若い男性が彼女に話しかけてきた。彼は彼女が知らない外国語を話した。彼女は「わかりません！　わかりません！」と言って彼から歩き去ろうとした。しかし彼は彼女についてきたので, 彼女は驚いた。彼女が彼から走って逃げようとしたとき, 彼は彼女の腕を触った。彼女は怖くなって彼を見た。彼はほほ笑んで彼女に財布を見せ, 彼女にそれを渡した。そのとき彼女はすべてを理解した。「ああ, 私は財布を落としたんだわ。彼はそれを見つけて, 私に返したかったんだわ」と彼女は思った。彼女は彼が何語を話したのかわからなかったが, 彼女は「どうもありがとう」と彼に言った。彼はまたほほ笑むと立ち去った。

Listen & Write!

ディクテーションにチャレンジしましょう！

I heard a story from one of my Japanese friends. It happened to her a month ago. When she was going to buy a train ticket at a station, her wallet was not in her bag. She looked for it for a (   ) but couldn't find it.

5 She didn't know (   ) to do. Suddenly a young man spoke to her. He spoke a foreign language she didn't (   ). She said, "No! No!" and tried to walk away from him. But he followed her, and she was surprised. When she tried to (   ) (   ) from him,

10 he touched her arm. She was afraid and looked at him. He smiled, showed her a wallet, and gave it to her. Then she understood (   ). "Oh, I dropped it. He found it and wanted to give it back to me," she thought. She didn't know what language he spoke, but she said to him,

15 "Thank you very much." He smiled again and walked away.

Read aloud!
音読しましょう！

I heard / a story / from one of my Japanese friends. / It happened /
私は聞いた　　ある話を　　　　私の日本人の友達の1人から　　　　　　それは起こった

to her / a month ago. / When she was going to buy / a train ticket /
彼女に　　　1カ月前に　　　　彼女が買おうとしたとき　　　　　電車の切符を

at a station, / her wallet / was not in her bag. / She looked for it /
駅で　　　　彼女の財布が　　　彼女のかばんの中になかった　　　彼女はそれを探した

for a while / but couldn't find it. / She didn't know / what to do. /
しばらく　　　しかしそれを見つけることができなかった　　彼女はわからなかった　　どうしたらよいのか

Suddenly / a young man / spoke to her. / He spoke / a foreign
突然　　　　若い男性が　　　彼女に話しかけてきた　　彼は話した　　外国語を

language / she didn't know. / She said, / "No! No!" / and tried /
彼女が知らない　　　　彼女は言った　「わかりません！わかりません！」そしてしようとした

to walk away / from him. / But he followed her, / and she was
歩き去ることを　　　彼から　　　しかし彼は彼女についてきた　　なので彼女は驚いた

surprised. / When she tried / to run away / from him, /
彼女がしようとしたとき　　走って逃げることを　　　彼から

he touched her arm. / She was afraid / and looked at him. /
彼は彼女の腕を触った　　　彼女は怖くなった　　　　そして彼を見た

He smiled, / showed her a wallet, / and gave it / to her. / Then /
彼はほほ笑んで　　　彼女に財布を見せた　　　そしてそれを渡した　彼女に　　そのとき

she understood everything. / "Oh, I dropped it. / He found it /
彼女はすべてを理解した　　　「ああ、私はそれを落としたんだわ　彼はそれを見つけて

and wanted to give it back / to me," / she thought. / She didn't
それを返したかったんだわ　　　　私に」　　と彼女は思った　　彼女はわからなかった

know / what language / he spoke, / but she said to him, /
何語を　　　　彼が話したのか　　　しかし彼女は彼に言った

"Thank you very much." / He smiled again / and walked away.
「どうもありがとう」　　　彼はまたほほ笑んだ　　　そして立ち去った

Listen & Write! (前ページの解答)

I heard a story from one of my Japanese friends. It happened to her a month ago. When she was going to buy a train ticket at a station, her wallet was not in her bag. She looked for it for a (**while**) but couldn't find it. She didn't know (**what**) to do. Suddenly a young man spoke to her. He spoke a foreign language she didn't (**know**). She said, "No! No!" and tried to walk away from him. But he followed her, and she was surprised. When she tried to (**run**) (**away**) from him, he touched her arm. She was afraid and looked at him. He smiled, showed her a wallet, and gave it to her. Then she understood (**everything**). "Oh, I dropped it. He found it and wanted to give it back to me," she thought. She didn't know what language he spoke, but she said to him, "Thank you very much." He smiled again and walked away.

Unit 9

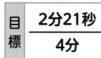
読む時間 | 目標 | **2分21秒**
解く時間 | | **4分**

1回目 ——————
2回目 ——————
3回目 ——————

Let's read!

次の英文は，海中のマイクロプラスチック（microplastics in the ocean）とレジ袋（Plastic Bags）についての，由紀（Yuki）と留学生のボブ（Bob）の会話です。これを読んで，あとの設問に答えなさい。

Yuki : I watched the news on TV last night. It was about microplastics in the ocean. ①(know) about microplastics?

Bob : Yes, I do. I know that a lot of people in many countries use and throw away plastics. I hear that much goes into
5 the sea and becomes smaller. The pieces are so small that we can't find them all.

Yuki : Microplastics are very small, but some people have seen them even in the Arctic Ocean.

Bob : Yes. Microplastics ②(find) all over the world. We can't take
10 all of them out of the ocean. We must do something about the problem.

Yuki : ③ (_____) We should reduce the plastics we use, and recycle more plastics. Do you have any ideas, Bob?

Bob : I think ④we can decrease the number of plastic bags we
15 use.

Yuki : That sounds good.

(長野県)

(注) throw away：捨てる　the Arctic Ocean：北極海　reduce：減らす

62

Questions

問1 本文の流れに合うように，下線部①，②の語を，必要があれば適切な形に変えたり不足している語を補ったりなどして，それぞれ最も適切な形に直して書きなさい。

問2 下線部③に入れるのに最も適切な英文をア～エの中から選びなさい。

ア．You did it.　イ．Are you OK?　ウ．What's this?　エ．You're right.

問3 次の英文が下線部④の具体例になるように，空所に入れるのに最も適切なものをア～エの中から1つ選びなさい。

When we buy something at the shop, we should say that (　　　).

ア．we want to use new plastic bags

イ．we won't need a plastic bag

ウ．we must get a new plastic bag

エ．we can't live without plastic bags

解答欄

問1	①		②	
問2		問3		

Answers

答えをチェックしましょう。

問1	①	Do you know	②	are found
問2	エ	問3	イ	

問1　① 文末の「？」（クエスチョンマーク）と，続くボブの発言 Yes, I do. から，Do you で始まる疑問文にすることがわかります。よって，Do you know が正解になります。

　　　② マイクロプラスチックは世界中で「見つけ<u>られる</u>」という関係。よって，「主語が…される」の関係となる**「be ＋動詞の過去分詞形」**の形，are found が正解になります。「Microplastics find」とすると「マイクロプラスチックが（何かを）見つける」となるので不自然です。

問2　直前のボブの発言「ぼくたちはその問題について何かをしなければいけない」に対して，ユキは空所直後に「私たちは，使用するプラスチックを減らして，より多くのプラスチックをリサイクルするべきよ」と，具体的な行動を提案しています。よって，ボブの発言に同意するエが正解となります。

〈選択肢の和訳〉
　　　× ア．あなたがそれをやった。
　　　× イ．大丈夫？
　　　× ウ．これは何？
　　　○ エ．そのとおり。

問3　「ぼくらが使うレジ袋の数を減らすことはできる」が下線部の意味です。つまり，店で買い物をするときに，レジ袋を受け取らないようにすれば，下線部の具体例を示す内容になると考えられます。よって，イが正解になります。

〈問題文・選択肢の和訳〉
　　　店で何かを買うとき，私たちは…と言うべきだ。
　　　× ア．新しいレジ袋を使いたい
　　　○ イ．レジ袋は必要ない
　　　× ウ．新しいレジ袋を手に入れなければならない
　　　× エ．レジ袋なしでは生活できない

Vocabulary

単語と意味を確認しましょう。

☐ watch	[wátʃ]	【動】見る
☐ last night		【熟】昨夜
☐ ocean	[óuʃən]	【名】〈the ～〉海
☐ a lot of ～		【熟】たくさんの～
☐ use	[júːz] [júːs]	【動】使う
☐ I hear that ...		【熟】…だそうだ
☐ much	[mʌ́tʃ]	【名】多く（のもの），たくさん
☐ go into the sea		【熟】海に流れ込む
☐ become smaller		【熟】より小さくなる
☐ piece	[píːs]	【名】破片
☐ so ... that ～		【熟】とても…なので～
☐ find	[fáind]	【動】見つける
☐ even	[íːvən]	【副】…でさえ
☐ all over the world		【熟】世界中で
☐ take ... out of ～		【熟】～から…を取り出す
☐ must	[məst]	【助】…しなければならない
☐ something	[sʌ́mθìŋ]	【代】何か
☐ problem	[prábləm]	【名】問題
☐ right	[ráit]	【形】正しい
☐ You're right.		【熟】〈相手の言うことなどに同意して〉そのとおり。
☐ should	[ʃúd]	【助】…すべきである
☐ recycle	[riːsáikəl]	【動】リサイクルする，再利用する
☐ idea	[aidíːə]	【名】アイデア，考え
☐ decrease	[dìːkríːs]	【動】減らす
☐ the number of ～		【名】～の数
☐ plastic bag		【名】レジ袋，ビニール袋
☐ That sounds good.		【熟】いいですね。

和訳例

Yuki：昨夜，テレビでニュースを見たの。海の中のマイクロプラスチックについてだったわ。あなたはマイクロプラスチックについて知っているかしら。

Bob：うん。多くの国々のたくさんの人たちがプラスチックを使ったり，捨てたりしていることを知っているよ。多くは海に流れ込んでより小さくなるそうだよ。その破片はとても小さいので，それらをすべてを見つけることはできないんだよ。

Yuki：マイクロプラスチックはとても小さいんだけど，中には北極海でさえ，それらを見た人がいるのよ。

Bob：そうなんだよ。マイクロプラスチックは世界中で見つけられるんだ。海からマイクロプラスチックのすべてを取り除くことなんてできない。ぼくたちはその問題について何かをしなければいけない。

Yuki：そのとおりよ。私たちは，使用するプラスチックを減らして，より多くのプラスチックをリサイクルするべきよ。何かアイデアはある，ボブ？

Bob：ぼくらが使うレジ袋の数を減らすことはできると思うよ。

Yuki：それはいいわね。

Unit 10

Listen & Write!

ディクテーションにチャレンジしましょう！

Yuki : I watched the news on TV last night. It was about microplastics in the ocean. Do you know about microplastics?

Bob : Yes, I do. I know that a lot of people in many countries
5   use and throw away plastics. I (   ) that much goes into the sea and becomes smaller. The pieces are so small that we (   ) find them all.

Yuki : Microplastics are very small, but some people have seen them even in the Arctic Ocean.

10 Bob : Yes. Microplastics are (   ) all over the world. We can't take all of them out of the ocean. We must do (   ) about the problem.

Yuki : You're right. We should reduce the plastics we use, and recycle more plastics. Do you have any ideas, Bob?

15 Bob : I think we can decrease the number of plastic bags we use.

Yuki : That (   ) good.

20

Read aloud!

音読しましょう！

Yuki : I watched the news / on TV / last night. / It was about microplastics /
ニュースを見たの　　　テレビで　　昨夜　　それはマイクロプラスチックについてだったわ

in the ocean. / Do you know / about microplastics? /
海の中の　　　あなたは知っているかしら　　マイクロプラスチックについて

Bob : Yes, I do. / I know / that a lot of people / in many countries /
うん　　　知っているよ　　たくさんの人たちが…ということを　　多くの国々の

use and throw away plastics. / I hear / that much goes into the sea /
プラスチックを使ったり，捨てたりしている　…だそうだよ　　多くは海に流れ込んでいる

and becomes smaller. / The pieces are so small / that we can't
そしてより小さくなる　　　　その破片はとても小さいので　　　それらすべてを見つける

find them all. /
ことはできないんだよ

Yuki : Microplastics are very small, / but some people have seen them /
マイクロプラスチックはとても小さい　　　だけど中にはそれらを見た人もいるのよ

even in the Arctic Ocean. /
北極海でさえ

Bob : Yes. / Microplastics are found / all over the world. / We can't take
そうなんだよ マイクロプラスチックは見つけられる　　世界中で　　ぼくたちは海からそれらの

all of them out of the ocean. / We must do something / about the
すべてを取り除くことなんてできないよ　　ぼくたちは何かをしなければいけない　　その問題について

problem. /

Yuki : You're right. / We should reduce the plastics / we use, /
そのとおりよ　　　私たちはプラスチックを減らすべきよ　　　私たちが使用する

and recycle more plastics. / Do you have any ideas, / Bob? /
そしてより多くのプラスチックをリサイクルするべきよ　何かアイデアはある　　　ボブ

Bob : I think / we can decrease / the number of plastic bags / we use. /
ぼくは思う　ぼくらは減らすことができる　　レジ袋の数を　　　ぼくらが使う

Yuki : That sounds good.
それはいいわね

Listen & Write! （前ページの解答）

Yuki : I watched the news on TV last night. It was about microplastics in the ocean. Do you know about microplastics?

Bob : Yes, I do. I know that a lot of people in many countries use and throw away plastics. I (**hear**) that much goes into the sea and becomes smaller. The pieces are so small that we (**can't**) find them all.

Yuki : Microplastics are very small, but some people have seen them even in the Arctic Ocean.

Bob : Yes. Microplastics are (**found**) all over the world. We can't take all of them out of the ocean. We must do (**something**) about the problem.

Yuki : You're right. We should reduce the plastics we use, and recycle more plastics. Do you have any ideas, Bob?

Bob : I think we can decrease the number of plastic bags we use.

Yuki : That (**sounds**) good.

Unit 10

67

Let's read!

次の英文は，ミエ（Mie）が自然体験キャンプについて書いたものです。これを読んで，あとの設問に答えなさい。

　　Last summer, I went to a camp in a village for a week. (1)<u>About twenty students and some teachers from different schools were there.</u> I enjoyed a lot of things with them.

　　The second day was the most exciting day for me.
5 (2)<u>We took care of animals on the farm, swam in the river, and watched stars at night.</u> We also cooked lunch.

　　I had to make a fire to cook lunch with Keiko. This was the first time for us. We got some firewood and tried to make a fire. But it wasn't so easy to do it. We asked our teacher for
10 help. He said, "Think and try. This is important in this camp." After thinking hard, we tried several ways. Then we thought, "Firewood needs air to burn! We have to think about the way to arrange the firewood." At last it burned. We were really happy. This was the most interesting thing for me.

15 　　I learned an important thing at this camp. When we have something to do, we should think and try hard. Then we will learn new things.

(和歌山県)

# Questions

問1 下線部 (1) を言いかえた英文として最も適切なものを選びなさい。

① There were twenty students and teachers altogether at the camp.

② There were twenty students and teachers from the same school at the camp.

③ There were less than twenty students and teachers at the camp.

④ There were over twenty students and teachers from different schools at the camp.

問2 下線部 (2) を言いかえた英文として最も適切なものを選びなさい。

① We had only one activity at the camp.

② We enjoyed various activities at the camp.

③ We didn't have any activities at night at the camp.

④ We enjoyed riding animals on the farm.

Unit 11

解答欄

問1		問2	

Answers

答えをチェックしましょう。

問1	④	問2	②

問1　「いろいろな学校からやってきた約 20 人の生徒と何人かの先生がそこにいた」が下線部の意味です。About twenty students and some teachers（約 20 人の生徒と何人かの先生）なので，合計 20 人以上いることが読み取れます。よって、④が正解となります。③の less than 〜（〜よりも少ない）や, ④の over 〜（〜を超える [〜以上]）は重要表現として覚えておきましょう。

〈選択肢の和訳〉

× ① そのキャンプには，合計で 20 人の生徒と教師がいた。

× ② そのキャンプには，同じ学校から 20 人の生徒と先生がやってきていた。

× ③ そのキャンプでは，生徒と先生は 20 人より少なかった。

○ ④ そのキャンプには，いろいろな学校からやってきた生徒と先生が 20 人以上いた。

問2　「私たちは農場で動物の世話をし，川で泳ぎ，夜には星を見た」が下線部の意味です。キャンプでさまざまな活動をしたことが読み取れるため，②が正解となります。また, この文では took, swam, watched という 3 つの動詞が並べて使われています。このように，3つ以上の要素を並べるときには, A, B, and C のように, カンマを使って並べ，最後の要素の前にのみ and や or を使います。

〈選択肢の和訳〉

× ① キャンプでは 1 つの活動しかしなかった。

○ ② キャンプではさまざまな活動を楽しんだ。

× ③ キャンプでは夜の活動はなかった。

× ④ 農場では動物に乗って楽しんだ。

重要な表現7

then の異なる意味

then は「そのとき，そのあとで」という意味で非常によく使われる副詞です。本文では 11 行目に **Then** we thought ...（そのあとで私たちは思った）のように使われています。ただし, 本文の最後の文 **Then** we will learn new things. の Then は, 直前の we should think and try hard（よく考えて一生懸命やってみるべきだ）を受けて,「そうすれば」という意味で使われています。

Vocabulary

単語と意味を確認しましょう。

☐ last	[lǽst]	【形】最後の, この前の	
☐ summer	[sʌ́mər]	【名】夏	
☐ camp	[kǽmp]	【名】キャンプ	
☐ village	[vílidʒ]	【名】村	
☐ for a week		【熟】1週間	
☐ twenty	[twénti]	【形】20の	
☐ some	[səm]	【形】いくらかの	
☐ different	[dífərənt]	【形】違った, いろいろな	
☐ school	[skúːl]	【名】学校	
☐ enjoy	[endʒɔ́i]	【動】楽しむ	
☐ second	[sékənd]	【形】第2の, 2番目の	
☐ most	[móust]	【副】最も, 一番	
☐ exciting	[iksáitiŋ]	【形】ワクワクする	
☐ took	[túk]	【動】take (する) の過去形	
☐ take care of ~		【熟】~の世話をする	
☐ animal	[ǽnəməl]	【名】動物	
☐ farm	[fɑ́ːrm]	【名】農場	
☐ swam	[swǽm]	【動】swim (泳ぐ) の過去形	
☐ star	[stɑ́ːr]	【名】星	
☐ at night		【熟】夜に (は)	
☐ also ...	[ɔ́ːlsou]	【副】…もまた	
☐ cook	[kúk]	【動】料理する	
☐ lunch	[lʌ́ntʃ]	【名】昼食	
☐ have to ...		【熟】…しなければならない	

☐ make a fire		【熟】火をおこす	
☐ got	[gɑ́t]	【動】get (得る) の過去形	
☐ firewood	[fáiərwùd]	【名】薪	
☐ try to ...		【熟】…しようと試みる	
☐ so	[sóu]	【副】〈否定文で〉それほど	
☐ easy	[íːzi]	【形】簡単な	
☐ ask A for B		【熟】A に B を求める	
☐ help	[hélp]	【名】助け, 手伝い	
☐ said	[séd]	【動】say(言う)の過去・過去分詞形	
☐ think	[θíŋk]	【動】思う, 考える	
☐ after ~	[ǽftər]	【前】~のあとで	
☐ hard	[hɑ́ːrd]	【副】一生懸命に, よく	
☐ several	[sévərəl]	【形】いくつかの	
☐ way	[wéi]	【名】方法	
☐ then	[ðén]	【副】そのとき, そうすれば	
☐ need	[níːd]	【動】必要とする	
☐ air	[éər]	【名】空気	
☐ burn	[bɑ́ːrn]	【動】燃える	
☐ arrange	[əréindʒ]	【動】並べる	
☐ at last		【熟】ついに	
☐ really	[ríːəli]	【副】本当に	
☐ learn	[lɑ́ːrn]	【動】習得する, 学ぶ	
☐ when ...	[hwén]	【接】…(する)ときに	
☐ something	[sʌ́mθiŋ]	【代】〈肯定文で〉何か	
☐ should ...	[ʃúd]	【助】…すべきである	

和訳例

　昨年の夏, 私は1週間ある村でのキャンプに出かけた。いろいろな学校からやってきた約20人の生徒と何人かの先生がそこにいた。私は彼らと一緒にたくさんのことを楽しんだ。

　2日目は私にとって一番ワクワクする日だった。私たちは農場で動物の世話をし, 川で泳ぎ, 夜には星を見た。私たちはお昼ご飯も作った。

　私はお昼ご飯を作るために, ケイコと一緒に火をおこさなければならなかった。これは私たちにとって初めてのことだった。私たちは薪を拾ってきて火をおこそうとした。しかし, そうすることはそんなに簡単ではなかった。私たちは先生に手伝ってくれるよう頼んだ。先生は, 「考えてやってみなさい。これがこのキャンプでは大切なんです」と言った。よく考えたあと, 私たちはいくつかの方法を試した。そのあとで私たちは, 「薪が燃えるには空気が必要だ！　私たちは薪を並べる方法について考えなければいけない」と思った。ついに薪は燃えた。私たちは本当にうれしかった。これが私には一番おもしろいことだった。

　私はこのキャンプで重要なことを学んだ。何かするべきことを持っているときは, よく考えて一生懸命やってみるべきだ。そうすれば私たちは新しいことを学ぶだろう。

Unit 11

Listen & Write!

ディクテーションにチャレンジしましょう！

Last summer, I went to a camp in a village for a week. About twenty students and some teachers from different schools were there. I enjoyed a lot of things with them.

The second day was the most exciting day for me. We
5 (   ) (   ) of animals on the farm, swam in the river, and watched stars at night. We also cooked lunch.

I had to (   ) a fire to cook lunch with Keiko. This was the first time for us. We got some firewood and
10 tried to make a fire. But it wasn't so easy to do it. We asked our teacher for (   ). He said, "Think and try. This is important in this camp." After thinking hard, we tried several ways. Then we thought, "Firewood needs air to burn! We have to think about the way to arrange the firewood."
15 (   ) (   ) it burned. We were really happy. This was the most interesting thing for me.

I learned an important thing at this camp. When we have something to do, we should think and try (   ). Then we will learn new things.

Read aloud!

音読しましょう！

Last summer, / I went to a camp / in a village / for a week. /
昨年の夏　　　　　　私はキャンプに出かけた　　　　ある村での　　　　　1週間

About twenty students / and some teachers / from different schools /
約20人の生徒　　　　　　そして何人かの先生が　　　　いろいろな学校から来た

were there. / I enjoyed / a lot of things / with them. /
そこにいた　　　私は楽しんだ　　たくさんのことを　　　彼らと一緒に

The second day / was the most exciting day / for me. / We took care /
2日目は　　　　　　一番ワクワクする日だった　　　私にとって　　私たちは世話をした

of animals / on the farm, / swam in the river, / and watched stars /
動物の　　　　農場で　　　　　川で泳いだ　　　　　そして星を見た

at night. / We also cooked lunch. /
夜に　　　　私たちはお昼ご飯も作った

I had to make a fire / to cook lunch / with Keiko. / This was /
私は火をおこさなければならなかった　　お昼ご飯を作るために　　ケイコと一緒に　　これは…だった

the first time / for us. / We got some firewood / and tried / to make
初めてのこと　　私たちにとって　　私たちは薪を拾った　　　そしてしようとした　火をおこすことを

a fire. / But / it wasn't so easy / to do it. / We asked our teacher /
　　　　　しかし　　そんなに簡単ではなかった　　そうすることは　　私たちは先生に頼んだ

for help. / He said, / "Think and try. / This is important / in this camp." /
手伝ってくれるよう　彼は言った　「考えてやってみなさい　　これが大切です　　　このキャンプでは」

After thinking hard, / we tried several ways. / Then we thought, /
よく考えたあと　　　　私たちはいくつかの方法を試した　　　そのあとで私たちは思った

"Firewood needs air / to burn! / We have to think / about the way /
「薪は空気が必要だ！　　燃えるには　私たちは考えなければいけない　　方法について

to arrange the firewood." / At last / it burned. / We were really happy. /
薪を並べるための」　　　　　ついに　　それは燃えた　　私たちは本当にうれしかった

This was / the most interesting thing / for me. /
これが…だった　　　一番おもしろいこと　　　　私には

I learned / an important thing / at this camp. / When we have / something
私は学んだ　　　重要なことを　　　　このキャンプで　　私たちが持っているとき　　何かするべきことを

to do, / we should think / and try hard. / Then / we will learn / new things.
私たちは考えて　　一生懸命やってみるべきだ　そうすれば　私たちは学ぶだろう　　新しいことを

Listen & Write! (前ページの解答)

　　Last summer, I went to a camp in a village for a week. About twenty students and some teachers from different schools were there. I enjoyed a lot of things with them.

　　The second day was the most exciting day for me. We (**took**) (**care**) of animals on the farm, swam in the river, and watched stars at night. We also cooked lunch.

　　I had to (**make**) a fire to cook lunch with Keiko. This was the first time for us. We got some firewood and tried to make a fire. But it wasn't so easy to do it. We asked our teacher for (**help**). He said, "Think and try. This is important in this camp." After thinking hard, we tried several ways. Then we thought, "Firewood needs air to burn! We have to think about the way to arrange the firewood." (**At**) (**last**) it burned. We were really happy. This was the most interesting thing for me.

　　I learned an important thing at this camp. When we have something to do, we should think and try (**hard**). Then we will learn new things.

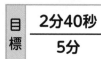

英文の長さ **160** words

	50	100	150	200

📖 読む時間
✏️ 解く時間

目標 | 2分40秒 / 5分

1回目 ——— 2回目 ——— 3回目 ———

Let's read!

次の英文と表は food mileage（フードマイレージ）について書かれたものです。これを読んで,あとの設問に答えなさい。

Have you ever thought about the food you eat every day? Where does it come from? How does it come to you?

A lot of food comes to Japan from many countries. And a lot of fuel is used when the food is carried to us from
5 other countries. Using too much fuel is not good for the environment.

The distance food moves is called food mileage. Food mileage tells us how much fuel we use when we send food to other countries. If the food mileage is higher, it is bad for the
10 environment. Look at the table below. Japan buys a lot of food from many countries. Japan's food mileage is higher than that of the other three countries. This means Japan is not kind to the environment. We need to think about this.

Buying locally produced food is a good way to help the
15 environment. So let's eat locally produced food and be kind to the environment.

Food mileage of four countries （単位：百万トンキロメートル）

Japan	South Korea	USA	UK
900.2	317.2	295.8	188.0

出典：フードマイレージキャンペーンのホームページ

（沖縄県）

（注）food mileage：「輸入される食料の重量×輸送距離」で計算される値

74

Questions

問1　本文の内容をまとめた次の英文の空所 (1) ～ (4) に入れるのに最も適切な語をア～
カから選びなさい。

　　　　Japan buys a lot of food from many countries.　So we use a lot of
fuel to (　1　) food from other countries.　Food mileage is the idea to be
(　2　) to the environment.　Japan's food mileage is the (　3　) of the four
countries.　For the environment, we should (　4　) locally produced food.

　　　ア. help　　イ. kind　　ウ. carry　　エ. eat　　オ. higher　　カ. highest

問2　本文の内容と一致するものを下のア～エの中から2つ選びなさい。
　　　ア. Japanese people eat a lot of food from many countries.
　　　イ. Eating locally produced food isn't good for the environment.
　　　ウ. The food mileage of the USA is higher than that of South Korea.
　　　エ. The food mileage of the UK isn't higher than that of the USA.

解答欄

問1	(1)		(2)		(3)		(4)	
問2								

Answers

答えをチェックしましょう。

問1	(1)	ウ	(2)	イ	(3)	カ	(4)	エ
問2	ア，エ							

問1 (1) 燃料を使うのは，食料を移動させるためなので，「運ぶ」という意味の carry が適切です。

(2) 直前の be 動詞や直後にある前置詞の to をヒントにして，形容詞の kind(優しい)を入れることができます。be kind to ～で「～に対して優しくする」という意味になります。

(3) データの中の数字から，日本のフードマイレージは4カ国の中で最も高いものとなっていることがわかります。また，空所の直前に the があることからも，最上級の highest が適切です。

(4) shouldという助動詞の直後なので，原形の動詞が続きます。選択肢の動詞の中で，前後の意味に最も自然に当てはまるのは，「～を食べる」という意味の eat です。

〈問題文の和訳〉

日本は多くの国からたくさんの食べ物を買っている。だから他の国々から食べ物を運ぶために私たちはたくさんの燃料を使っている。フードマイレージは環境に優しくなろうという考え方である。日本のフードマイレージは4カ国の中で最も高い。環境のために，私たちは地元で生産される食べ物を食べるべきだ。

問2 選択肢の正解・不正解の理由は以下のようになります。

ア．3行目の A lot of food comes to Japan from many countries.（たくさんの食べ物が多くの国々から日本にやってくる）という文に一致しています。

イ．15～16行目に「地元で生産される食べ物を食べて環境に優しくなろう」とあるので，この選択肢はその逆となり，本文と矛盾します。

ウ．表ではアメリカのフードマイレージの数値は韓国よりも低くなっています。

エ．表の数値では，イギリスのフードマイレージのほうがアメリカよりも低くなっているので，この文は表のデータと一致しています。

〈選択肢の和訳〉

○ ア．日本人は多くの国々からやってきた食べ物をたくさん食べる。

× イ．地元で生産される食べ物を食べることは環境によくない。

× ウ．アメリカのフードマイレージは韓国のフードマイレージよりも高い。

○ エ．イギリスのフードマイレージはアメリカのフードマイレージよりも高くない。

Vocabulary

単語と意味を確認しましょう。

□ ever	[évər]	【副】〈疑問文で〉今までに	
□ think about ~		【熟】~について考える	
□ food	[fúːd]	【名】食べ物	
□ eat	[íːt]	【動】食べる	
□ every day		【熟】毎日	
□ come from ~		【熟】~から来る	
□ how	[háu]	【副】どのようにして, どれくらい	
□ come to ~		【熟】~のところに来る	
□ a lot of ~		【熟】多くの~	
□ Japan	[dʒəpǽn]	【名】日本	
□ many	[méni]	【形】多くの	
□ country	[kʌ́ntri]	【名】国	
□ fuel	[fjúːəl]	【名】燃料	
□ use	[júːz]	【動】使う	
□ when ...	[hwén]	【接】…(する)ときに	
□ carry	[kǽri]	【動】運ぶ	
□ other	[ʌ́ðər]	【形】他の	
□ too	[túː]	【副】あまりにも, (限度を) すぎて	
□ environment	[enváiərənmənt]	【名】環境	
□ distance	[dístəns]	【名】距離	
□ move	[múːv]	【動】動く, 移動する	
□ call	[kɔ́ːl]	【動】呼ぶ	
□ tell	[tél]	【動】示す, 伝える	
□ send	[sénd]	【動】送る	

□ if ...	[if]	【接】もし…ならば	
□ higher	[háiər]	【形】high (高い) の比較級	
□ look at ~		【熟】~を見る	
□ table	[téibəl]	【名】テーブル, 表	
□ below	[bilóu]	【副】下に [の]	
□ buy	[bái]	【動】買う	
□ mean	[míːn]	【動】意味する, 表す	
□ kind	[káind]	【形】親切な, 優しい	
□ need to ...		【熟】…する必要がある	
□ locally	[lóukəli]	【副】地元で, 特定の場所で	
□ produce	[prədjúːs]	【動】生産する	
□ way	[wéi]	【名】方法	
□ help	[hélp]	【動】救う, 助ける	
□ so ...	[sóu]	【接】だから…	
□ South Korea	[sáuθ kəríːə]	【名】韓国	
□ USA		【名】アメリカ (the United States (of America))	
□ UK		【名】イギリス (the United Kingdom of Great Britain and Northern Ireland)	

和訳例

　あなたは今までに毎日自分が食べる食べ物について考えたことがあるだろうか。それは, どこから来るのだろうか。それは, どのようにしてあなたのところにくるのだろうか。

　たくさんの食べ物が多くの国々から日本にやってくる。また, 食べ物が他の国々から私たちのところまで運ばれるとき, たくさんの燃料が使われる。燃料をたくさん使いすぎることは, 環境にとってよくない。

　食べ物が移動する距離はフードマイレージと呼ばれる。フードマイレージは, 私たちが他の国々に食べ物を送るときにどれだけ多くの燃料を使うのかを示している。もしフードマイレージがより高ければ, 環境にはよくない。下の表を見てみよう。日本は多くの食べ物を多くの国々から買っている。日本のフードマイレージは他の3つの国のものよりも高い。これは日本が環境に対して優しくないということを意味している。私たちはこのことについて考える必要がある。

　地元で生産される食べ物を買うことは, 環境を救うためのよい方法である。だから, 地元で生産される食べ物を食べて環境に優しくなろう。

Unit 12

Listen & Write!

ディクテーションにチャレンジしましょう！

Have you ever thought about the food you eat every day? Where does it come from? How does it come to you?

A lot of food comes to Japan from many countries. And a lot of fuel is used when the food is (   ) to

5 us from other countries. (   ) too much fuel is not good for the environment.

The distance food moves is called food mileage. Food mileage tells us (   ) (   ) fuel we use when we send food to other countries. If the food mileage is

10 higher, it is bad for the environment. Look at the table below. Japan buys a lot of food from many countries. Japan's food mileage is higher than that of the other three countries. This means Japan is not (   ) to the environment. We need to think about this.

15 (   ) locally produced food is a good way to help the environment. So let's eat locally produced food and be kind to the environment.

Read aloud!

音読しましょう！

Have you ever / thought about the food / you eat / every day? /
あなたは今までにあるだろうか　　食べ物について考えたことが　　自分が食べる　　毎日

Where / does it come from? / How / does it come / to you? /
どこから　　それは来るのだろうか　　どのようにして　それは来るのだろうか　あなたのところに

A lot of food comes / to Japan / from many countries. /
たくさんの食べ物がやってくる　　日本に　　多くの国々から

And a lot of fuel / is used / when the food is carried / to us from other
また，たくさんの燃料が　　使われる　　食べ物が運ばれるとき　　他の国々から私たちのところまで

countries. / Using too much fuel / is not good / for the environment. /
燃料をたくさん使いすぎることは　　よくない　　環境にとって

The distance / food moves / is called food mileage. / Food mileage /
距離は　　食べ物が移動する　　フードマイレージと呼ばれる　　フードマイレージは

tells us / how much fuel / we use / when we send food /
私たちに示している　　どれだけ多くの燃料を　私たちが使うのか　　私たちが食べ物を送るときに

to other countries. / If the food mileage / is higher, / it is bad /
他の国々に　　もしフードマイレージが　　より高ければ　　それはよくない

for the environment. / Look at the table / below. / Japan buys /
環境には　　表を見てみよう　　下の　　日本は買っている

a lot of food / from many countries. / Japan's food mileage / is higher /
多くの食べ物を　　多くの国々から　　日本のフードマイレージは　　より高い

than that of the other three countries. / This means / Japan is not
他の3つの国のものよりも　　これは意味している　　日本は優しくない

kind / to the environment. / We need to / think about this. /
環境に対して　　私たちはする必要がある　　このことについて考えることを

Buying locally produced food / is a good way / to help the
地元で生産される食べ物を買うことは　　よい方法である　　環境を救うための

environment. / So let's eat / locally produced food / and be kind /
だから，食べよう　　地元で生産される食べ物を　　そして優しくなろう

to the environment.
環境に

Listen & Write! (前ページの解答)

Have you ever thought about the food you eat every day? Where does it come from? How does it come to you?

A lot of food comes to Japan from many countries. And a lot of fuel is used when the food is (**carried**) to us from other countries. (**Using**) too much fuel is not good for the environment.

The distance food moves is called food mileage. Food mileage tells us (**how**)(**much**) fuel we use when we send food to other countries. If the food mileage is higher, it is bad for the environment. Look at the table below. Japan buys a lot of food from many countries. Japan's food mileage is higher than that of the other three countries. This means Japan is not (**kind**) to the environment. We need to think about this.

(**Buying**) locally produced food is a good way to help the environment. So let's eat locally produced food and be kind to the environment.

Unit 12

Unit 13

50 100 150 200

英文の長さ 166 words

読む時間 目標 2分46秒
解く時間 5分

1回目 ——— 2回目 ——— 3回目 ———

Let's read!

次の英文は，「樹医」（木の医者）であった山野忠彦氏について書かれたものです。これを読んで，あとの設問に答えなさい。

　Tadahiko Yamano spent most of his life as a tree doctor. He could talk with trees in Japan.

　Before World War II he worked in the mountains. During the war few people took care of the (1), and so a lot of trees became sick. He heard their cries for help. And he decided to (2) a tree doctor. He thought it was his life's work to help sick trees.

　He (3) how to take care of such trees by himself. Then he visited different places in Japan. He helped a lot of trees by giving them fertilizer, medicine, and other things. Some of them were more than 300 years old. There were many famous trees, too.

　People often say, "Some trees are healthy, and some are not." But Mr. Yamano said, "All trees have their own good points. I hope (4) tree will become stronger and stronger." Mr. Yamano had a very (5) heart and he took care of many sick trees all over Japan.

(和歌山県)

(注) by himself：自分で　　fertilizer：肥料

80

Questions

問1 空所（1）〜（5）に入れるのに最も適切な語をそれぞれ下のア〜エの中から1つずつ選びなさい。

(1) ア．rivers　　イ．forests　　ウ．villages　　エ．cities

(2) ア．become　　イ．see　　ウ．love　　エ．believe

(3) ア．forgot　　イ．taught　　ウ．learned　　エ．exchanged

(4) ア．no　　イ．every　　ウ．one　　エ．another

(5) ア．small　　イ．cold　　ウ．young　　エ．warm

問2 本文の内容と一致する英文を2つ選びなさい。

① Mr. Yamano understood the languages of animals.

② Mr. Yamano worked as a doctor before World War Ⅱ.

③ Many trees became sick during the war.

④ Mr. Yamano thought it was his life's work to grow trees.

⑤ Mr. Yamano didn't like to use fertilizer and medicine.

⑥ Mr. Yamano sometimes treated very old trees.

⑦ Mr. Yamano hoped that he would be stronger and stronger.

解答欄

問1	(1)		(2)		(3)		(4)		(5)	
問2										

Unit 13

Answers

答えをチェックしましょう。

問1	(1)	イ	(2)	ア	(3)	ウ	(4)	イ	(5)	エ
問2	③，⑥									

問1 (1) この話全体は「樹医（木の医者）」の活動について書かれています。空所の直前にある熟語，take care of ～は「～の世話をする」という意味です。木の医者が何の世話をするのかと考えると，「イ」の forests（森）が最も適切だとわかります。

× ア. 川　　　　　○イ. 森　　　　× ウ. 村　　　　× エ. 都市

(2) decide to ... は「…することに決める」という意味です。直後の a tree doctor と意味的に結びつく動詞を選びます。become ～は「～になる」という意味で，これを入れると意味が通ります。

○ ア. ～になる　　× イ. ～が見える　× ウ. ～を愛する　× エ. ～を信じる

(3) 直後の how to ... は「どのように…するか，…する方法」という意味です。木の医者になるためには，「木々の世話をする方法」を「学ぶ」わけですから，learn（学ぶ）という動詞が適切だと考えることができます。

× ア. ～を忘れた　　× イ. ～を教えた　○ ウ. ～を学んだ　× エ. ～を交換した

(4) 直前の文に All trees have their own good points.（すべての木にはそれぞれよいところがある）と書いてあることから，空所にも，all と似たような形容詞が入るだろうと考えます。そこで every（あらゆる～）が適切です。every の直後には単数名詞が続きます。

× ア. 1つの～もない　　○ イ. あらゆる～　　× ウ. 1つの～　　× エ. もう1つの～

(5) 本文全体の内容から，山野氏は木に対して愛情あふれる人物であったことがわかります。そのような愛情深さを表すために，heart の直前に置く形容詞としては warm（温かい）が適切です。

× ア. 小さな　　　× イ. 冷たい　　× ウ. 若い　　　○ エ. 温かい

問2 3〜5行目「戦争の間は森を世話した人はほとんどいなかった，そのため多くの木々が病気になった」から③，また，10〜11行目「そうした木々のいくつかは，樹齢300年を超えていた」から⑥が正解とわかります。

〈選択肢の和訳〉

① 山野氏は動物の言葉を理解していた。

② 山野氏は第2次世界大戦の前に医者として働いていた。

③ 戦時中，多くの木々が病気になった。

④ 木を育てることが自分の一生の仕事だと，山野氏は思っていた。

⑤ 山野氏は肥料や薬を使うのが好きではなかった。

⑥ 山野氏はときどき，かなりの老木を治療することもあった。

⑦ 山野氏は，自分がますます強くなることを願っていた。

82

Vocabulary

単語と意味を確認しましょう。

□ spent	[spént]	【動】	spend（〈時間を〉過ごす）の過去・過去分詞形
□ most	[móust]	【名】	大部分，大半
□ as ~	[əz]	【前】	~として
□ tree doctor		【名】	樹医
□ could ...	[kúd]	【助】	can（…できる）の過去形
□ talk with ~		【熟】	~と話し合う
□ World War Ⅱ		【名】	第2次世界大戦
□ work	[wə́:rk]	【動】	働く
□ during ~	[djúəriŋ]	【前】	~の間
□ war	[wɔ́:r]	【名】	戦争
□ few	[fjú:]	【形】	ほとんどない
□ people	[pí:pəl]	【名】	人々
□ take care of ~		【熟】	~の世話をする
□ forest	[fɔ́(:)rəst]	【名】	森林
□ (and) so ...		【接】	だから…
□ a lot of ~		【熟】	多くの~
□ sick	[sík]	【形】	病気の
□ heard	[hə́:rd]	【動】	hear（聞く）の過去・過去分詞形
□ cry for help		【名】	助けを求める叫び
□ decide to ...		【熟】	…することに決める
□ life's work		【名】	一生の仕事
□ help	[hélp]	【動】	助ける
□ learn	[lə́:rn]	【動】	学ぶ，習得する
□ how to ...		【熟】	…する方法
□ such	[sʌ́tʃ]	【形】	そのような
□ visit	[vízət]	【動】	訪れる
□ different	[dífərənt]	【形】	違った，さまざまな
□ give	[gív]	【動】	与える
□ medicine	[médəsən]	【名】	薬
□ some	[sʌ́m]	【代】	いくつかのもの
□ more than ~		【熟】	~より多い，~以上
□ famous	[féiməs]	【形】	有名な
□ too	[tú:]	【副】	〈肯定文で〉…もまた
□ some	[sʌ́m]	【形】	いくつかの
□ healthy	[hélθi]	【形】	健康な
□ own	[óun]	【形】	自分自身の
□ good points		【名】	よいところ，長所
□ hope	[hóup]	【動】	望む
□ stronger	[strɔ́(:)ŋgər]	【形】	strong（強い）の比較級
□ stronger and stronger		【熟】	ますます強く
□ heart	[há:rt]	【名】	心，心臓
□ all over ~		【熟】	~じゅうの，~の至るところで

和訳例

　山野忠彦氏は，彼の人生の大半を樹医として過ごした。彼は日本の木々と話すことができた。第2次世界大戦の前は，彼は山の中で働いていた。戦争の間，森を世話した人はほとんどいなかった，そのため多くの木々が病気になった。彼は木々の助けを求める叫びを聞いた。そこで彼は樹医になることを決めた。彼は病気の木々を助けることが自分の一生の仕事だと考えたのだ。

　彼はそのような（病気の）木々の世話をする方法を自分1人で学んだ。それから，彼は日本のさまざまな場所を訪れた。彼は肥料や薬，その他の物を与えることで多くの木々を助けた。そうした木々のいくつかは，樹齢300年を超えていた。また，有名な木々もたくさんあった。

　人々はよく，「健康な木もあれば，そうでない木もある」と言う。だが山野氏は，「すべての木にそれぞれよいところがある。私はどの木もますます強くなってくれることを望んでいる」と言った。山野氏はとても温かい心を持ち，日本中のたくさんの病気の木々の世話をした。

Unit 13

Listen & Write!

ディクテーションにチャレンジしましょう！

Tadahiko Yamano spent most of his life as a tree doctor. He could talk with trees in Japan.

Before World War II, he worked in the mountains. During the war (   ) people took care of the forests, and
5 so a lot of trees became sick. He (   ) their cries for help. And he decided to become a tree doctor. He thought it was his life's work to help sick trees.

He learned how to take care of such trees (   ) (   ). Then he visited different
10 places in Japan. He helped a lot of trees by giving them fertilizer, medicine, and other things. Some of them were (   ) (   ) 300 years old. There were many famous trees, too.

People often say, "Some trees are healthy, and some
15 are not." But Mr. Yamano said, "All trees have their (   ) good points. I hope every tree will become stronger and stronger." Mr. Yamano had a very warm heart and he took care of many sick trees all over Japan.

Read aloud!

音読しましょう！

Tadahiko Yamano / spent most of his life / as a tree doctor. /
山野忠彦氏は　　　　　　彼の人生の大半を過ごした　　　　　　樹医として

He could talk / with trees in Japan. /
彼は話すことができた　　日本の木々と

Before World War II / he worked / in the mountains. /
第2次世界大戦の前は　　　　　　彼は働いていた　　　　　山の中で

During the war / few people / took care of the forests, /
戦争の間　　　　人はほとんどいない　　　　　森を世話した

and so a lot of trees / became sick. / He heard their cries / for help. /
そのため多くの木々が　　　病気になった　　彼は木々の叫びを聞いた　　助けを求める

And he decided / to become a tree doctor. / He thought /
そこで彼は決めた　　　　樹医になることを　　　　　彼は考えた

it was his life's work / to help sick trees. /
彼の一生の仕事だと　　　病気の木々を助けることが

He learned / how to take care / of such trees / by himself. / Then /
彼は学んだ　　　世話をする方法を　　そのような木々の　　自分1人で　　それから

he visited different places / in Japan. / He helped / a lot of trees /
彼はさまざまな場所を訪れた　　　日本の　　彼は助けた　　多くの木々を

by giving them / fertilizer, / medicine, / and other things. / Some of them /
それらに与えることによって　　肥料　　　薬　　　そしてその他の物を　　そうした木々のいくつかは

were more than 300 years old. / There were / many famous trees, / too. /
樹齢300年を超えていた　　　　　　あった　　　たくさんの有名な木々　　　もまた

People often say, / "Some trees / are healthy, / and some are not." / But
人々はよく言う　　　「いくつかの木は　　健康である　　そしていくつかの木はそうでない」

Mr. Yamano said, / "All trees / have their own good points. / I hope / every
だが山野氏は言った　「すべての木に　　それぞれよいところがある　　私は望んでいる　どの木も

tree / will become stronger and stronger." / Mr. Yamano / had a very
樹も　　ますます強くなってくれることを」　　　山野氏は　　　とても温かい心を

warm heart / and he took care / of many sick trees / all over Japan.
持っていた　　　そして彼は世話をした　　たくさんの病気の木々の　　　日本中の

Listen & Write! （前ページの解答）

　Tadahiko Yamano spent most of his life as a tree doctor. He could talk with trees in Japan.
　Before World War II he worked in the mountains. During the war (**few**) people took care of the forests, and so a lot of trees became sick. He (**heard**) their cries for help. And he decided to become a tree doctor. He thought it was his life's work to help sick trees.
　He learned how to take care of such trees (**by**) (**himself**). Then he visited different places in Japan. He helped a lot of trees by giving them fertilizer, medicine, and other things. Some of them were (**more**) (**than**) 300 years old. There were many famous trees, too.
　People often say, "Some trees are healthy, and some are not." But Mr. Yamano said, "All trees have their (**own**) good points. I hope every tree will become stronger and stronger." Mr. Yamano had a very warm heart and he took care of many sick trees all over Japan.

Unit 13

85

Unit 14

英文の長さ **196** words

50　100　150　200

読む時間　目標　**3分16秒**　　1回目　——————
解く時間　　　　**6分**　　　　2回目　——————
　　　　　　　　　　　　　　　　3回目　——————

Let's read!

次の英文を読み，あとの設問に答えなさい。

　　Apiwat is thirteen years old. He lives in a small village on the side of a mountain. He has lived in the village with his family since he was born. There is a tropical rain forest around the village. Apiwat likes the village and the forest around it.

5　　The forest was once large and beautiful, and the village was a quiet, happy place. Apiwat always played in the forest with his friends. Together they ran after small animals. They watched the animals and the birds and listened to them.

　　But one day many people came to the forest. (A) (① started, 10 ② a lot, ③ tall, ④ of, ⑤ they ⑥ cutting down, ⑦ trees) and they carried them away. After only a short time, the forest around the village began to disappear. Apiwat could not play there with his friends anymore.

　　Now there are only a few trees and the rain is washing 15 all the rich soil down the mountain into the river. New trees cannot grow. (B) (① moved away, ② the animals, ③ to, ④ of, ⑤ most, ⑥ and the birds, ⑦ have already, ⑧ other mountains). The forest around the village is becoming a desert. The village people think they have to do something to save the forest.

（岩手県）

（注）Apiwat：アピワト（男の子の名前）　tropical rain forest：熱帯雨林　soil：土

 **Questions**

問1　下の英文は本文の内容を話の順序に従ってまとめたものです。空所 (1) 〜 (3) に入れるのに最も適切な 1 語を，本文中から抜き出して書きなさい。

Apiwat has been in a small village for thirteen years.

He likes the (　1　) around the village.　He always played there.

A lot of (　2　) came there and cut down many trees.

The village people think they have to do something to save the forest because it looks like a (　3　) now.

問2　下線部（A）と（B）を意味の通る英文になるように，数字を使って並べかえなさい。なお，文頭も小文字で示してあります。

解答欄

問1	(1)		(2)		(3)	
問2	(A)					
	(B)					

Answers

答えをチェックしましょう。

問1	(1)	forest	(2)	people	(3)	desert
問2	(A)	⑤ – ① – ⑥ – ② – ④ – ③ – ⑦				
	(B)	⑤ – ④ – ② – ⑥ – ⑦ – ① – ③ – ⑧				

問1 (1) 4行目と6〜7行目で，Apiwat は村の周りの森が好きで，よくそこで遊んでいたことが述べられています。したがって，この空所には <u>forest</u> という単語が入ると考えられます。

(2) 本文には many people came to the forest と書いてあります。<u>many</u> は「多くの」という意味ですが，これは <u>a lot of</u> とも言いかえることができます。空所に <u>people</u> を入れると，本文と同じ意味を表すことができます。

(3) <u>look like ～</u>は「〜のように見える」という意味です。本文の最後のほうに，森が砂漠化していることが書いてあるので，この空所には，「砂漠」という意味の名詞，<u>desert</u> を入れると意味が通ります。

問2 (A) まず，主語と述語動詞を見つけることと，確実に前後がつながる表現を見つけてみましょう。主語になるのは <u>they</u>，述語動詞になるのは <u>started</u> です。a lot of ～（たくさんの〜）という熟語も先に見つけてつなげましょう。この文での cutting は動名詞で，started cutting down で「切り倒すことを始めた」という意味になります。

(B) <u>most of ～</u>は「ほとんどの〜」という意味の表現で，この most がこの文の主語になります。「**have already ＋過去分詞**」は，「もうすでに…してしまっている」という意味の現在完了形の表現なので，have already moved away が述語になるとわかります。

重要な表現⑧

時を表す表現に注意して読む

まとまった文章を読むときは，「いつ」のことなのか，「時」や「時の経過」を表す表現に注意すると，話の流れをとらえやすくなります。本文の第1段落では Apiwat **is** … や He **lives in** … などの現在形の動詞，また He **has lived** … という現在完了形から，**現時点**でのことを伝えているとわかります。同じように be 動詞や現在完了形に注目すると，第2段落と第3段落では**過去**のこと，第4段落では**現在**のことが述べられているとわかります。このほか，第2段落の **once**（かつて），第4段落の **now**（今）など，時を示す副詞も，「いつ」を示すキーワードです。

Vocabulary

単語と意味を確認しましょう。

☐ live	[lív]	【動】住む	
☐ village	[vílidʒ]	【名】村	
☐ side	[sáid]	【名】わき, 斜面	
☐ mountain	[máuntən]	【名】山	
☐ family	[fǽməli]	【名】家族	
☐ since ...	[síns]	【接】…して以来	
☐ be born		【熟】生まれる	
☐ forest	[fɔ́(ː)rəst]	【名】森林	
☐ around ~	[əráund]	【前】~の周囲に	
☐ once	[wʌ́ns]	【副】かつて	
☐ beautiful	[bjú:təfəl]	【形】美しい	
☐ quiet	[kwáiət]	【形】静かな	
☐ always	[ɔ́:lweiz]	【副】いつも	
☐ play	[pléi]	【動】遊ぶ	
☐ together	[təgéðər]	【副】一緒に	
☐ ran	[rǽn]	【動】run (走る) の過去形	
☐ run after ~		【熟】~を追いかける	
☐ animal	[ǽnəməl]	【名】動物	
☐ watch	[wátʃ]	【動】見る	
☐ bird	[bə́:rd]	【名】鳥	
☐ listen to ~		【熟】~を聞く	
☐ one day		【熟】ある日	
☐ many	[méni]	【形】多くの	
☐ people	[pí:pəl]	【名】人々	
☐ come to ~		【熟】~に来る	
☐ start	[stá:rt]	【動】始める	

☐ cut down		【熟】切り倒す	
☐ a lot of ~		【熟】多くの~	
☐ tall	[tɔ́:l]	【形】高い	
☐ tree	[trí:]	【名】木	
☐ carry away		【熟】運び去る	
☐ began	[bigǽn]	【動】begin(始める)の過去形	
☐ disappear	[dìsəpíər]	【動】消える, なくなる	
☐ could ...	[kúd]	【助】can(…できる)の過去形	
☐ anymore	[ènimɔ́:r]	【副】もはや	
☐ rain	[réin]	【名】雨	
☐ wash down		【熟】洗い流す	
☐ rich	[rítʃ]	【形】豊かな	
☐ grow	[gróu]	【動】育つ, 成長する	
☐ most	[móust]	【名】大部分	
☐ move away		【熟】立ち去る	
☐ other	[ʌ́ðər]	【形】他の	
☐ become	[bikʌ́m]	【動】~になる	
☐ desert	[dézərt]	【名】砂漠	
☐ think	[θíŋk]	【動】思う, 考える	
☐ have to ...		【熟】…しなければならない	
☐ something	[sʌ́mθiŋ]	【代】〈肯定文で〉何か	
☐ save	[séiv]	【動】救う	

和訳例

　アピワトは 13 歳だ。彼は山の斜面にある小さな村に住んでいる。彼は生まれたときから家族と一緒にその村に住んでいる。村の周囲には熱帯雨林がある。アピワトはその村とその周囲の森が好きだ。

　森は, かつては広くて美しく, 村は静かで幸せな場所だった。アピワトはいつも森の中で友達と遊んだ。彼らは一緒に小さな動物を追いかけた。彼らは動物や鳥を見たり, それらの声を聞いたりした。

　しかし, ある日, たくさんの人々が森にやってきた。彼らはたくさんの高い木を切り倒し始め, その木々を持ち去っていった。ほんの短い期間のあとに, 村の周りの森がなくなり始めた。アピワトはもはや, そこで友達と遊ぶことができなくなった。

　今, 木々はほんのわずかしかなく, 雨がすべての豊かな土を山から川へと洗い流している。新しい木は育つことができない。ほとんどの動物や鳥たちは, すでに他の山々へと立ち去ってしまった。村の周囲の森は砂漠になりつつある。村の人々は, 森林を救うために何かしなければならないと考えている。

Apiwat is thirteen years old. He lives in a small village on the side of a mountain. He has lived in the village with his family (   ) he was born. There is a tropical rain forest around the village. Apiwat likes the village and the

5 forest around it.

The forest was (   ) large and beautiful, and the village was a quiet, happy place. Apiwat always played in the forest with his friends. Together they ran after small animals. They watched the animals and the birds and listened

10 to them.

But (   ) (   ) many people came to the forest. They started cutting down a lot of tall trees and they carried them away. After only a short time, the forest around the village began to disappear. Apiwat could not play

15 there with his friends (   ).

Now there are only a few trees and the rain is washing all the rich soil down the mountain into the river. New trees cannot grow. (   ) of the animals and the birds have already moved away to other mountains. The forest

20 around the village is becoming a desert. The village people think they have to do something to save the forest.

Read aloud!
音読しましょう！

Apiwat / is thirteen years old. / He lives / in a small village / on the
アピワトは　　　13歳だ　　　彼は住んでいる　　　小さな村に　　　斜面の
side of / a mountain. / He has lived / in the village / with his family /
山の　　　彼は住んでいる　　　その村に　　　家族と一緒に
since he was born. / There is / a tropical rain forest / around the village. /
彼が生まれたときから　　ある　　　熱帯雨林が　　　村の周囲に
Apiwat likes / the village / and the forest around it. /
アピワトは好きだ　　その村が　　そしてその周囲の森が
　　The forest / was once large and beautiful, / and the village / was a quiet, /
森は　　　かつては広くて美しかった　　　そして村は　　　静かで
happy place. / Apiwat always played / in the forest / with his friends. /
幸せな場所だった　　アピワトはいつも遊んだ　　森の中で　　彼の友達と
Together / they ran after small animals. / They watched / the animals /
一緒に　　　彼らは小さな動物を追いかけた　　　彼らは見た　　　動物を
and the birds / and listened to them. /
そして鳥を　　　そしてそれらの声を聞いた
　　But one day / many people / came to the forest. / They started /
しかし，ある日　　たくさんの人々が　　森にやってきた　　彼らは始めた
cutting down / a lot of tall trees / and they carried them away. / After only
切り倒すことを　　たくさんの高い木を　　そしてそれらを持ち去っていった　　ほんの短い
a short time, / the forest / around the village / began to disappear. / Apiwat /
期間のあとに　　森は　　　村の周りの　　　なくなり始めた　　アピワトは
could not play there / with his friends / anymore. /
そこで遊ぶことができなかった　　彼の友達と　　もはや
　　Now there are only a few trees / and the rain / is washing / all the
今，木々はほんのわずかしかない　　　そして雨が　　流している　　すべての豊かな
rich soil / down the mountain / into the river. / New trees / cannot grow. /
土を　　　山を下って　　　川へと　　　新しい木は　　育つことができない
Most of the animals / and the birds / have already moved away /
ほとんどの動物　　そして鳥たちは　　すでに立ち去ってしまった
to other mountains. / The forest / around the village / is becoming a desert. /
他の山々へ　　　森は　　　村の周囲の　　　砂漠になりつつある
The village people think / they have to do something / to save the forest.
村の人々は考えている　　彼らは何かをしなければならない　　森林を救うために

Listen & Write! (前ページの解答)

Apiwat is thirteen years old. He lives in a small village on the side of a mountain. He has lived in the village with his family (**since**) he was born. There is a tropical rain forest around the village. Apiwat likes the village and the forest around it.

The forest was (**once**) large and beautiful, and the village was a quiet, happy place. Apiwat always played in the forest with his friends. Together they ran after small animals. They watched the animals and the birds and listened to them.

But (**one**)(**day**) many people came to the forest. They started cutting down a lot of tall trees and they carried them away. After only a short time, the forest around the village began to disappear. Apiwat could not play there with his friends (**anymore**).

Now there are only a few trees and the rain is washing all the rich soil down the mountain into the river. New trees cannot grow. (**Most**) of the animals and the birds have already moved away to other mountains. The forest around the village is becoming a desert. The village people think they have to do something to save the forest.

Unit 15

| 50 | 100 | 150 | 200 |

英文の長さ | 169 words |

読む時間 | 目標 | 2分49秒
解く時間 | | 4分

1回目 ———— 2回目 ———— 3回目 ————

Let's read!

次の英文を読み，あとの設問に答えなさい。

Miki : Mr. Nakata, (A) (<u>know, the, do, who, shortest, you, wrote, letter</u>) in the world?

Mr. Nakata : No, I don't. Who wrote it?

Miki : Victor Hugo did. Have you heard of him?

5 Mr. Nakata : Yes. He is a famous writer. How short was his letter?

Miki : He only wrote a question mark. He sent it to the publisher of his new book.

Mr. Nakata : What did Hugo want to say in the letter?

Miki : If you want to know (1)<u>that</u>, you will have to read
10   another short letter. It was a reply written by the publisher.

Mr. Nakata : What did the publisher write in the reply?

Miki : He wrote an exclamation mark. Do you understand now?

15 Mr. Nakata : Oh, yes. (2)<u>When Hugo read the reply, he became very happy</u>. Right?

Miki : That's right! The publisher wanted to say, "Many people are buying your new book. They are enjoying it!"

Mr. Nakata : Now I know what the question mark means. Hugo
20   wanted to say, " [＿＿＿＿＿＿] "

(高知県)

(注) Victor Hugo：ビクトル・ユゴー（フランスの作家で，名作『レ・ミゼラブル』の作者）
writer：作家　question mark：クエスチョンマーク（？）　publisher：発行者
reply：返信　exclamation mark：エクスクラメーションマーク（！）

Questions

問1　下線部 (A) を意味の通る英文になるように並べかえなさい。

問2　下線部 (1) の that が指しているものを，下のア～エの中から1つ選びなさい。
　　ア．ビクトル・ユゴーの職業
　　イ．ビクトル・ユゴーが新しい本を書いた時期
　　ウ．ビクトル・ユゴーが手紙を書いた相手
　　エ．ビクトル・ユゴーの手紙の意味

問3　下線部 (2) とほぼ同じ意味になるように，次の英文の空所に入れるのに最も適切な語を書きなさい。
　　The reply (　　　) Hugo very happy.

問4　英文最後の空所に入れるのに，最も適切な文を下のア～エの中から1つ選びなさい。
　　ア．Are many people buying my new book?
　　イ．Have you finished writing a new book?
　　ウ．Who wrote the shortest letter in the world?
　　エ．What do you want to say in your letter?

解答欄

問1	

問2		問3		問4	

Answers

答えをチェックしましょう。

問1	do you know who wrote the shortest letter				
問2	エ	問3	made	問4	ア

問1 次のナカタ先生の発言 No, I don't. がヒントです。これから Yes/No の答えを求める「**Do you ＋動詞の原形？**」（あなたは…しますか）という疑問文だとわかります。ここは最初に Mr. Nakata という呼びかけがあるので，do you know ...? で始め，「…を」の部分（目的語）を続けます。この文では，「世界で一番短い手紙を書いたのは誰か」という疑問文 Who wrote the shortest letter in the world?　全体が目的語になります。この who を使った疑問文（疑問詞が主語の疑問文）はそのまま目的語として使えるので，know のあとに続ければ文の完成です。

問2 <u>that</u> は前文の内容を指すことができます。よって，ここでは What did Hugo want to say in the letter?（ユゴーはその手紙で何を言いたかったんだろう）を指すとわかるので，エが正解です。

問3 下線部の意味は「返信を読んだとき，ユゴーはとても喜んだ」になります。よって，問題文を「その返信がユゴーをとても喜ばせた」となる英文にすれば，ほぼ同じ意味になります。空所は主語の後ろなので動詞が入ります。ここでは，重要表現「**主語＋ make A B**」（〜が A を B にする，〜のおかげで A は B になる）を使えばよいので，make を過去形にした <u>made</u> が正解とわかります。

問4 直前のミキの発言がヒントです。The publisher wanted to say, "Many people are buying your new book. ..." という発言に対してナカタ先生が「もう私はその疑問符が何を意味するかわかる」と述べ，続いて空所の発言をしています。よって，ミキの発言を疑問文にしたものが空所に入るので，アが正解です。ユゴーの手紙の場合は「your → my」のように代名詞を置きかえる必要がある点に注意しましょう。

〈選択肢の和訳〉

　　○ ア．多くの人が私の新しい本を買っているでしょうか。

　　× イ．あなたは新しい本を書き終えましたか。

　　× ウ．誰が世界で一番短い手紙を書きましたか。

　　× エ．あなたが手紙の中で言いたいことは何ですか。

Vocabulary

単語と意味を確認しましょう。

□ know	[nóu]	【動】知っている	
□ who	[hú:]	【代】誰が	
□ wrote	[róut]	【動】write（書く）の過去形（write - wrote - written）	
□ shortest	[ʃɔ́:rtəst]	【形】short（短い）の最上級	
□ letter	[létər]	【名】手紙	
□ in the world		【熟】世界中で	
□ heard	[hə́:rd]	【動】hear（聞く）の過去・過去分詞形	
□ hear of ～		【熟】～のうわさを聞く	
□ famous	[féiməs]	【形】有名な	
□ how	[háu]	【副】どのくらい	
□ sent	[sént]	【動】send（送る）の過去・過去分詞形	
□ want to ...		【熟】…したいと思う	

□ say	[séi]	【動】言う	
□ if ...	[if]	【接】もし…ならば	
□ have to ...		【熟】…しなければならない	
□ read	[rí:d]	【動】読む	
□ another	[ənʌ́ðər]	【形】もう1つの	
□ understand	[ʌ̀ndərstǽnd]	【動】理解する, わかる	
□ when ...	[hwén]	【接】…（する）ときに	
□ became	[bikéim]	【動】become（～になる）の過去形	
□ right	[ráit]	【間投】そうですよね 【形】正しい	
□ many	[méni]	【形】多くの	
□ people	[pí:pəl]	【名】人々	
□ buy	[bái]	【動】買う	
□ enjoy	[endʒɔ́i]	【動】楽しむ	
□ mean	[mí:n]	【動】意味する	

和訳例

Miki：世界で一番短い手紙を書いたのは誰か知っていますか，ナカタ先生。

Mr. Nakata：いや，知らない。誰が書いたんだい。

Miki：ビクトル・ユゴーです。彼のことを聞いたことがありますか。

Mr. Nakata：ああ。彼は有名な作家だね。彼の手紙はどのくらい短かったの？

Miki：彼は疑問符（？）だけを書きました。彼はその手紙を彼の新しい本の発行者に送りました。

Mr. Nakata：ユゴーはその手紙で何を言いたかったんだろうか。

Miki：それが知りたければ，別の短い手紙を読まなければならないでしょう。それは発行者によって書かれた返信でした。

Mr. Nakata：発行者は返信で何を書いたのかな。

Miki：彼は感嘆符（！）を書きました。もうわかりますか。

Mr. Nakata：ああ，わかった。ユゴーがその返信を読んだとき，彼はとても喜んだ。そうだろう？

Miki：そのとおりです！　発行者は「多くの人があなたの新しい本を買っています。彼らはその本を楽しんでいます！」と言いたかったのです。

Mr. Nakata：もうその疑問符が何を意味するかわかるよ。ユゴーは「多くの人が私の新しい本を買っていますか」と言いたかったんだね。

Listen & Write!

ディクテーションにチャレンジしましょう！

Miki :	Mr. Nakata, do you know who wrote the shortest letter in the world?
Mr. Nakata :	No, I don't. Who wrote it?
Miki :	Victor Hugo ( ). Have you heard of him?
5 Mr. Nakata :	Yes. He is a famous writer. How short was his letter?
Miki :	He ( ) wrote a question mark. He sent it to the publisher of his new book.
Mr. Nakata :	What did Hugo want to say in the letter?
Miki :	If you want to know that, you will have to read another short letter. It was a reply ( ) by the publisher.
Mr. Nakata :	What did the publisher write in the reply?
Miki :	He wrote an exclamation mark. Do you understand now?
15 Mr. Nakata :	Oh, yes. When Hugo ( ) the reply, he became very happy. Right?
Miki :	That's right! The publisher wanted to say, "Many people are buying your new book. They are enjoying it!"
20 Mr. Nakata :	( ) I know what the question mark means. Hugo wanted to say, "Are many people buying my new book?"

Read aloud!

音読しましょう！

Miki : Mr. Nakata, / do you know / who wrote the shortest letter / in the world? /
ナカタ先生　　知っていますか　　一番短い手紙を書いたのは誰か　　　世界で

Mr. Nakata : No, I don't. / Who wrote it? /
いや，知らない　誰がそれを書いたんだい

Miki : Victor Hugo did. / Have you heard of him? /
ビクトル・ユゴーです　　彼のことを聞いたことがありますか

Mr. Nakata : Yes. / He is a famous writer. / How short / was his letter? /
ああ　　彼は有名な作家だね　　どのくらい短かったの　　彼の手紙は

Miki : He only wrote a question mark. / He sent it / to the publisher /
彼は疑問符だけを書きました　　　　彼はそれを送りました　　発行者に

of his new book. /
彼の新しい本の

Mr. Nakata : What / did Hugo want to say / in the letter? /
何を　　ユゴーは言いたかったんだろうか　　その手紙で

Miki : If you want / to know that, / you will have to read /
もしあなたが…したければ　　それを知ることを　　あなたは読まなければならないでしょう

another short letter. / It was a reply / written / by the publisher. /
別の短い手紙を　　　それは返信でした　　書かれた　　発行者によって

Mr. Nakata : What / did the publisher write / in the reply? /
何を　　　発行者は書いたのか　　　返信で

Miki : He wrote an exclamation mark. / Do you understand now? /
彼は感嘆符を書きました　　　　もうわかりますか

Mr. Nakata : Oh, yes. / When Hugo / read the reply, / he became very happy. / Right? /
ああ，わかった　ユゴーが…とき　その返信を読んだ　　彼はとても喜んだ　　そうだろう

Miki : That's right! / The publisher wanted to say, / "Many people /
そのとおりです　　　　発行者は言うことを望んだ　　　　「多くの人が

are buying your new book. / They are enjoying it!" /
あなたの新しい本を買っています　　彼らはそれを楽しんでいます」

Mr. Nakata : Now I know / what the question mark means. / Hugo wanted to say, /
もう私はわかる　　その疑問符が何を意味するか　　　　ユゴーは言いたかった

"Are many people / buying my new book?"
「たくさんの人が　　私の新しい本を買っていますか」と

Listen & Write! (前ページの解答)

Miki : Mr. Nakata, do you know who wrote the shortest letter in the world?
Mr. Nakata : No, I don't. Who wrote it?
Miki : Victor Hugo (**did**). Have you heard of him?
Mr. Nakata : Yes. He is a famous writer. How short was his letter?
Miki : He (**only**) wrote a question mark. He sent it to the publisher of his new book.
Mr. Nakata : What did Hugo want to say in the letter?
Miki : If you want to know that, you will have to read another short letter. It was a reply (**written**) by the publisher.
Mr. Nakata : What did the publisher write in the reply?
Miki : He wrote an exclamation mark. Do you understand now?
Mr. Nakata : Oh, yes. When Hugo (**read**) the reply, he became very happy. Right?
Miki : That's right! The publisher wanted to say, "Many people are buying your new book. They are enjoying it!"
Mr. Nakata : (**Now**) I know what the question mark means. Hugo wanted to say, "Are many people buying my new book?"

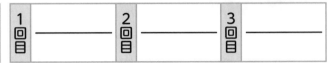

英文の長さ **178** words

| | | 50 | 100 | 150 | 200 |

📖 読む時間　目標 **2分58秒**
✏️ 解く時間　目標 **5分30秒**

| 1回目 | ——— | 2回目 | ——— | 3回目 | ——— |

Let's read!

次の英文を読んで，あとの設問に答えなさい。

Why are there so many hungry people in the world? I think that food loss is one of the reasons. Do you know a lot of food is lost and
5 wasted in the world each year?

Why do people lose and waste so much food? (1), in developed countries, farmers throw away a lot of fruits and vegetables when their size or color is not good for selling. In developing countries, people
10 throw away a lot of food because they can't keep them in good condition. (2), most food thrown away goes bad and produces greenhouse gases. It is another big problem.

Look at this graph. Before I found this graph, I thought there was much more industrial food loss than food loss from
15 homes. But when I looked at it, I was surprised. It shows that (3). It means that we can do something. If we reduce food loss in our homes, we can make a big difference. Let's make the world a better place.

(鳥取県)

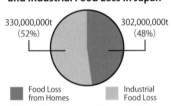

The Amount of Food Loss from Homes and Industrial Food Loss in Japan

330,000,000t (52%)　　302,000,000t (48%)

■ Food Loss from Homes　■ Industrial Food Loss

「農林水産省　食品ロスの削減とリサイクルの推進に向けて（平成28年7月）」より作成

(注) food loss：廃棄される食品　　wasted：waste（無駄にする）の過去分詞形
developed country：先進国　　farmer：農業者　　condition：状態　　go bad：腐る
much：はるかに　　industrial food loss：事業所等で廃棄される食品　　reduce：減らす
amount：量

98

Questions

問1 空所 (1)，(2) に入れるのに最も適切な語（句）をそれぞれ 1 つずつ選びなさい。

(1)　ア．For the first time
　　　イ．Before that
　　　ウ．For example
　　　エ．In the end

(2)　ア．Also
　　　イ．But
　　　ウ．First
　　　エ．Actually

問2 空所 (3) に入れるのに最も適切な英文を下のア～エの中から選びなさい。
　　ア．industrial food loss is smaller than food loss from homes
　　イ．industrial food loss is much larger than food loss from homes
　　ウ．food loss from homes is almost twice the amount of industrial food loss
　　エ．food loss from homes is almost as large as industrial food loss

解答欄

問1	(1)		(2)		問2	

Answers

答えをチェックしましょう。

問1	(1)	ウ	(2)	ア	問2	エ

問1　(1) 直前の文「なぜ人はこんなにも多くの食べ物を失い，無駄にするのでしょうか」
　　　　　という疑問に対し，空所の直後ではその理由の具体的な例を示しています。よっ
　　　　　て，具体的な例を示すウが正解とわかります。

　　〈選択肢の和訳〉
　　　　× ア．はじめて　× イ．その前に　○ ウ．例えば　× エ．最終的に

　　　(2) 空所に続く文「捨てられた食品の大部分は腐り，温室効果ガスを発生させます。
　　　　　それは別の大きな問題です」から，空所以降は「捨てられた食品がもたらす別な
　　　　　問題」が述べられていることがわかります。よって，情報を追加する働きのアが
　　　　　正解とわかります。

　　〈選択肢の和訳〉
　　　　○ ア．また　　　× イ．しかし　　× ウ．第一に　× エ．実際は

問2　この段落の1文目に「このグラフを見てください」とあるため，It shows that ... の
　　　It はグラフを指していて，ここはその内容を答える問題だとわかります。グラフを見
　　　ると，事業所等で廃棄される食品は52%，家庭で廃棄される食品は48%であるこ
　　　とがわかり，両者はほぼ同じ量であることが読み取れます。よって，エが正解とわ
　　　かります。as ... as ～で「～と同じくらい…だ」という意味を表します。

　　〈選択肢の和訳〉
　　　　× ア．事業所等で廃棄される食品は家庭で廃棄される食品よりも少ない
　　　　× イ．事業所等で廃棄される食品は家庭で廃棄される食品よりもはるかに多い
　　　　× ウ．家庭で廃棄される食品は事業所等で廃棄される食品のほぼ2倍の量である
　　　　○ エ．家庭で廃棄される食品は事業所等で廃棄される食品とほぼ同じ量である

Vocabulary

単語と意味を確認しましょう。

☐ hungry	[hʌ́ŋgri]	【形】	飢えた，空腹の
☐ one of the -s		【名】	〜の１つ
☐ reason	[ríːzən]	【名】	理由，わけ
☐ a lot of 〜		【熟】	多く［たくさん］の〜
☐ lost	[lɔ(ː)st]	【動】	lose（なくす，失う）の過去・過去分詞形
☐ each	[íːtʃ]	【形】	毎〜，各〜
☐ for example		【熟】	例えば
☐ throw away 〜		【熟】	〜を捨てる
☐ vegetable		【名】	野菜
☐ be good for selling		【熟】	販売に適している
☐ developing country		【名】	発展途上国
☐ keep 〜 in good condition		【熟】	〜をよい状態に保つ
☐ also	[ɔ́ːlsou]	【副】	また，その上
☐ most	[móust]	【形】	大部分の
☐ produce	[prədjúːs]	【動】	生じさせる，生産する
☐ greenhouse gas		【名】	温室効果ガス
☐ another	[ənʌ́ðər]	【形】	もう１つの，別の
☐ problem	[prábləm]	【名】	問題
☐ look at 〜		【熟】	〜を見る
☐ graph	[grǽf]	【名】	グラフ，表
☐ found	[fáund]	【動】	find（見つける）の過去・過去分詞形
☐ thought		【動】	think（思う，考える）の過去・過去分詞形
☐ be surprised		【熟】	驚く
☐ It shows that ...		【熟】	それは…と示している
☐ almost	[ɔ́ːlmoust]	【副】	ほとんど，ほぼ
☐ It means that ...		【熟】	それは…を意味する［示している］
☐ make a big difference		【熟】	大きな違いをもたらす
☐ make A B		【熟】	A を B にする

Unit 16

和訳例

　なぜ世界にはこんなにも多くの飢えた人々がいるのでしょうか。私は，廃棄される食品がその理由の１つだと考えています。毎年，世界では多くの食品が失われ，無駄にされていることを知っていますか。

　なぜ人はこんなにも多くの食品を失い，無駄にするのでしょうか。例えば，先進国では，大きさや色が販売に適さないとき，農業者は多くの果物や野菜を捨ててしまいます。発展途上国では，食品をよい状態に保つことができないため，人々は多くの食品を捨てています。また，捨てられた食品の大部分は腐り，温室効果ガスを発生させます。それは別の大きな問題です。

　このグラフを見てください。このグラフを見つける前は，家庭で廃棄される食品よりも事業所等で廃棄される食品のほうがはるかに多いと私は思っていました。しかし，それを見て，私は驚きました。家庭で廃棄される食品は，事業所等で廃棄される食品とほぼ同じ量であることを，それは示しています。それは，私たちに何かができるということです。私たちが家庭で廃棄される食品を減らせば，大きな違いをもたらすことができます。世界をよりよい場所にしましょう。

Listen & Write!

ディクテーションにチャレンジしましょう!

Why are there so many (   ) people in the world? I think that food loss is one of the reasons. Do you know a lot of food is lost and wasted in the world each year?

Why do people lose and waste so much food? For example, in
5 developed countries, farmers throw away a lot of fruits and vegetables when their size or color is not (   ) for selling. In developing countries, people throw away a lot of food because they can't keep them in good condition. Also, most food thrown away goes bad and produces greenhouse gases. It is (   ) big
10 problem.

Look at this graph. Before I found this graph, I thought there was much more industrial food loss than food loss from homes. But when I looked at it, I was surprised. It shows that food loss from homes is almost as (   ) as industrial food loss. It means that
15 we can do something. If we reduce food loss in our homes, we can (   ) a big difference. Let's make the world a better place.

Read aloud!

音読しましょう！

Why are there / so many hungry people / in the world? / I think /
なぜいるのでしょうか　　こんなにも多くの飢えた人々が　　　　世界には　　　私は考えています

that food loss is one of the reasons. / Do you know / a lot of food is lost /
廃棄される食品がその理由の１つだと　　　　知っていますか　　多くの食品が失われていることを

and wasted / in the world / each year? /
そして無駄にされていることを 世界で　　　毎年

Why do people lose / and waste / so much food? / For example, /
なぜ人々は失うのでしょうか　そして無駄にするのでしょうか こんなにも多くの食品を　　　例えば

in developed countries, / farmers throw away / a lot of fruits and vegetables /
先進国では　　　　　　農業者は捨ててしまいます　　　多くの果物や野菜を

when their size or color is not good / for selling. / In developing countries, /
それらの大きさや色が適さないとき　　　　販売するのに　　　　発展途上国では

people throw away a lot of food / because they can't keep them /
人々は多くの食品を捨てています　　　　なぜならそれらを保つことができないため

in good condition. / Also, / most food / thrown away / goes bad /
よい状態に　　　　また　　大部分の食品は　　捨てられた　　　腐り

and produces greenhouse gases. / It is another big problem. /
そして温室効果ガスを発生させます　　　　それは別の大きな問題です

Look at this graph. / Before I found this graph, / I thought / there
このグラフを見てください　　このグラフを見つける前は　　　私は思っていました　…があると

was / much more industrial food loss / than food loss from homes. / But /
はるかに多くの事業所等で廃棄される食品が　　　　家庭で廃棄される食品よりも　　　しかし

when I looked at it, / I was surprised. / It shows / that food loss from homes /
それを見て　　　　私は驚きました　　それは示しています　　家庭で廃棄される食品は

is almost as large / as industrial food loss. / It means / that we can do
ほぼ同じ量であることを　　事業所等で廃棄される食品と　　それは示しています　　私たちに何かができる

something. / If we reduce food loss / in our homes, / we can make a big
ということを　　　もし私たちが廃棄される食品を減らせば　　家庭で　　　私たちは大きな違いをもたらす

difference. / Let's make the world a better place.
ことができます　　　　世界をよりよい場所にしましょう

Listen & Write! （前ページの解答）

Why are there so many (hungry) people in the world? I think that food loss is one of the reasons. Do you know a lot of food is lost and wasted in the world each year?

Why do people lose and waste so much food? For example, in developed countries, farmers throw away a lot of fruits and vegetables when their size or color is not (good) for selling. In developing countries, people throw away a lot of food because they can't keep them in good condition. Also, most food thrown away goes bad and produces greenhouse gases. It is (another) big problem.

Look at this graph. Before I found this graph, I thought there was much more industrial food loss than food loss from homes. But when I looked at it, I was surprised. It shows that food loss from homes is almost as (large) as industrial food loss. It means that we can do something. If we reduce food loss in our homes, we can (make) a big difference. Let's make the world a better place.

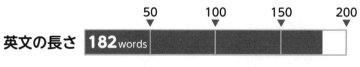

Unit 17

英文の長さ **182** words

50   100   150   200

読む時間 ／ 解く時間

目標	3分2秒		1回目		2回目		3回目	
	12分							

Let's read!

次の英文はナオミ（Naomi）と彼女の兄と父がドライブした ときの話です。これを読んで，あとの設問に答えなさい。

Naomi lives with her parents and her brother.

One day, Naomi's father went to the lake and her brother went to the sea in their own cars. They left their house at the same time, 9 o'clock in the morning. Her father drove his car

5 to the west at a speed of 60 km/h, and her brother went to the east at a speed of 80 km/h.

Naomi wanted to visit her grandfather. So she went together with her brother. She got out of the car at 9:45 in the morning and walked 2 km to the west to his house.

10 The distances from Naomi's home to her father's and brother's destinations were the same. Her brother arrived at the sea at 11 o'clock in the morning. Later, her father arrived at the lake.

Naomi's father and brother started for home from the lake

15 and the sea at the same time. They drove at the same speeds as they did in the morning, but her brother took a break at a hamburger shop. At last, they came home at the same time.

（国立高専 改）

（注）west：西　～km/h：時速～キロメートル（kilometer per hour と読む）
　　　east：東　distance：距離　destination：目的地

Questions

問 本文の内容に合うように，下の1〜4の英文の空所に入れるのに最も適切なものを
ア〜エの中からそれぞれ1つずつ選びなさい。なお，道はすべて直線であるものとし，
自動車の乗降および加減速に要する時間は考慮しないこととします。

1. At 9:30 in the morning, the distance between the two cars was (   ).
   ア. 22 km   イ. 50 km   ウ. 70 km   エ. 100 km

2. The distance between Naomi's house and her grandfather's was (   ).
   ア. 43 km   イ. 47 km   ウ. 58 km   エ. 62 km

3. At 11:00 in the morning, Naomi's father had to drive another (   )
   to the lake.
   ア. 30 minutes   イ. 40 minutes   ウ. 50 minutes   エ. 60 minutes

4. Naomi's brother stayed at the hamburger shop for (   ).
   ア. 20 minutes   イ. 30 minutes   ウ. 40 minutes   エ. 60 minutes

解答欄

1		2		3		4	

Answers

答えをチェックしましょう。

| 1 | ウ | 2 | ウ | 3 | イ | 4 | ウ |

1. 3〜4行目に「出発したのは午前9時」とあるので，30分後（1/2h）の距離を考えればいいことがわかります。続けて「父は西へ時速60kmで移動」（60km/h × 1/2h = 30km），「兄は東へ時速80kmで移動」（80km/h × 1/2h = 40km）とありますので，求める距離は「30km + 40km = 70km」となります。

   〈問題文の和訳〉

   「午前9時30分に，2台の車の間の距離は（　　　　）だった」

2. 5〜9行目から，「ナオミは兄と一緒に東へ時速80kmで移動し，45分後（3/4h）に下車」（80km/h × 3/4h = 60km），そこから「西（東とは逆方向）へ2km歩いた」（− 2km）とわかります。したがって，求める距離は「60km − 2km = 58km」となります。

   〈問題文の和訳〉

   「ナオミの家と彼女の祖父の家との距離は（　　　　）だった」

3. 10〜11行目から，「ナオミの家から父と兄の目的地までの距離は同じ」だとわかります。続けて「兄が（目的地の）海に到着したのは午前11時（出発から2時間後）」（80km/h × 2h = 160km）から，目的地までの距離は160kmだとわかります。父は「時速60kmで移動」（2時間（2h）で120km）ということがわかるので，湖までの残りの距離は「160km − 120km = 40km」となります。時間は「道のり÷速さ」で計算できますので，「40km ÷ 60km/h」で2/3h，つまり父が目的地までかかる時間はあと40分となります（父の移動時間は全部で2時間40分となります）。

   〈問題文の和訳〉

   「午前11時に，ナオミの父は湖まであと（　　　　）運転しなければならなかった」

4. 最終段落から，2台の車は同時に出発して同時に家に到着したことがわかります。父の車の移動時間は，設問の3からもわかるように，2時間40分です。兄の車の所要時間は2時間なので，その差の40分間，兄はハンバーガーショップにいたことがわかります。

   〈問題文の和訳〉

   「ナオミの兄は（　　　　）間，ハンバーガーショップにいた」

Vocabulary

単語と意味を確認しましょう。

□ live with 〜		【熟】〜と一緒に住む	
□ parents	[péərənts]	【名】両親	
□ brother	[bríðər]	【名】兄, 弟	
□ one day		【熟】ある日	
□ father	[fá:ðər]	【名】父	
□ went	[wént]	【動】go (行く) の過去形	
□ lake	[léik]	【名】湖	
□ sea	[sí:]	【名】海	
□ own	[óun]	【形】自分自身の	
□ car	[ká:r]	【名】車	
□ left	[léft]	【動】leave (出発する) の過去・過去分詞形	
□ at the same time		【熟】同時に	
□ in the morning		【熟】朝に, 午前中に	
□ drove	[dróuv]	【動】drive (運転する) の過去形	
□ to the west		【熟】西に	
□ at a speed of 60 km/h		【熟】時速60kmで	

□ to the east		【熟】東に	
□ want to ...		【熟】…したいと思う	
□ visit	[vízət]	【動】訪れる	
□ grandfather	[grǽndfà:ðər]	【名】祖父	
□ so ...	[sóu]	【接】だから…	
□ together	[təgéðər]	【副】一緒に	
□ get out of the car		【熟】車から降りる	
□ walk	[wɔ́:k]	【動】歩く	
□ from A to B		【熟】A から B まで	
□ arrive at 〜		【熟】〜に到着する	
□ later	[léitər]	【副】あとで, その後	
□ start for 〜		【熟】〜に向けて出発する	
□ as ...	[ǽz]	【接】(…する) ように	
□ but ...	[bʌ́t]	【接】しかし…	
□ take a break		【熟】休憩する	
□ hamburger shop		【名】ハンバーガーショップ	
□ at last		【熟】最終的に	

Unit 17

和訳例

ナオミは両親と兄と一緒に住んでいる。

ある日, それぞれ自分の車で, ナオミの父は湖へ行き, 兄は海へ行った。彼らは午前9時に同時に家を出発した。彼女の父は時速60kmのスピードで西へ向かって車を運転し, 兄は時速80kmのスピードで東に向かった。

ナオミは祖父を訪ねたかった。だから彼女は兄と一緒に行った。彼女は午前9時45分に車を降りて, 祖父の家まで西の方向へ2km歩いた。

ナオミの家から, 父と兄の目的地までの距離は同じだった。兄は午前11時に海に着いた。その後, 父は湖に着いた。

ナオミの父と兄は湖と海から同時に家へ向かって出発した。彼らは午前中にしたのと同じスピードで運転したが, 兄はハンバーガーショップで休憩をとった。最終的に, 彼らは同時に家に着いた。

Naomi lives with her parents and her brother.

One day, Naomi's father went to the lake and her brother went to the sea in their own cars. They (   ) their house at the same time, 9 o'clock in the morning. Her father

5 (   ) his car to the west at a speed of 60 km/h, and her brother went to the east at a speed of 80 km/h.

Naomi wanted to (   ) her grandfather. So she went together with her brother. She got out of the car at 9:45 in the morning and walked 2 km to the west to his house.

10   The distances from Naomi's home to her father's and brother's destinations were the same. Her brother arrived at the sea at 11 o'clock in the morning. Later, her father arrived at the lake.

Naomi's father and brother (   ) for home

15 from the lake and the sea at the same time. They drove at the same speeds as they did in the morning, but her brother took a (   ) at a hamburger shop. At last, they came home at the same time.

Read aloud!

音読しましょう！

Naomi lives / with her parents / and her brother. /
ナオミは住んでいる　　　両親と一緒に　　　　　そして兄と

One day, / Naomi's father / went to the lake / and her brother / went to
ある日　　　　ナオミの父は　　　湖へ行った　　　　そして兄は　　　海へ行った

the sea / in their own cars. / They left their house / at the same time, /
　　　　それぞれ自分の車で　　　彼らは家を出発した　　　　同時に

9 o'clock in the morning. / Her father / drove his car / to the west /
午前9時に　　　　　　　　　彼女の父は　　車を運転した　　西へ向かって

at a speed / of 60 km/h, / and her brother / went to the east /
スピードで　　時速60km の　　　そして兄は　　　東に向かった

at a speed of 80 km/h. /
時速80km のスピードで

Naomi wanted / to visit her grandfather. / So she went together /
ナオミはしたかった　　祖父を訪ねることを　　だから彼女は一緒に行った

with her brother. / She got out of the car / at 9:45 in the morning /
兄と　　　　　　彼女は車を降りた　　　　午前9時45分に

and walked 2 km / to the west / to his house. /
そして2km歩いた　　西の方向へ　　彼の家まで

The distances / from Naomi's home / to her father's and brother's
距離は　　　　　ナオミの家から　　　　父と兄の目的地までの

destinations / were the same. / Her brother arrived / at the sea / at 11
目的地の　　　　同じだった　　　　兄は着いた　　　　海に　　　11時に

o'clock / in the morning. / Later, / her father / arrived at the lake. /
午前の　　　　　　その後　　　父は　　　　湖に着いた

Naomi's father and brother / started for home / from the lake /
ナオミの父と兄は　　　　　家へ向かって出発した　　　湖から

and the sea / at the same time. / They drove / at the same speeds /
そして海から　　　　同時に　　　　彼らは運転した　　　同じスピードで

as they did / in the morning, / but her brother / took a break /
彼らがしたように　　午前中に　　　しかし彼女の兄は　　　休憩を取った

at a hamburger shop. / At last, / they came home / at the same time.
ハンバーガーショップで　　最終的に　　彼らは家に着いた　　　同時に

Listen & Write! (前ページの解答)

Naomi lives with her parents and her brother.

One day, Naomi's father went to the lake and her brother went to the sea in their own cars. They (**left**) their house at the same time, 9 o'clock in the morning. Her father (**drove**) his car to the west at a speed of 60 km/h, and her brother went to the east at a speed of 80 km/h.

Naomi wanted to (**visit**) her grandfather. So she went together with her brother. She got out of the car at 9:45 in the morning and walked 2 km to the west to his house.

The distances from Naomi's home to her father's and brother's destinations were the same. Her brother arrived at the sea at 11 o'clock in the morning. Later, her father arrived at the lake.

Naomi's father and brother (**started**) for home from the lake and the sea at the same time. They drove at the same speeds as they did in the morning, but her brother took a (**break**) at a hamburger shop. At last, they came home at the same time.

 ## Let's read!

次の英文を読んで，あとの設問に答えなさい。

Have you （ A ） thought about your future? When I am asked, I always say, "I'd like to be a firefighter." For me, (1) it is an exciting and important job.

When I was ten years old, I saw a movie about firefighters.
5 I was moved when I saw how they rescued people in the movie. I decided that I wanted to be a firefighter. I wanted to know many things about firefighters.

The next day, I asked my teacher about firefighters. She told me to go to the Fire Museum in Tokyo. When I went to
10 the museum with my father, a woman （ B ） worked there said to me, "Of course, firefighters put out fires, but (2) (how, fires, they also, people, to, teach, prevent)."

I learned a lot of things from the movie and the woman at the museum. Now I know that helping people is very
15 important. And so, (3)I want to be a firefighter.

(千葉県)

(注) future：将来   firefighter：消防士   was moved：感動した   rescue：救う
the Fire Museum：消防博物館   put out fires：火事を消す   prevent：防ぐ

110

Questions

問1　空所 (A) に入れるのに最も適切な語を書きなさい。

問2　下線部 (1) が指しているものを日本語で書きなさい。

問3　空所 (B) に入れるのに最も適切な語を書きなさい。

問4　下線部 (2) の語（句）を正しい英文になるように並べかえなさい。

問5　筆者が下線部 (3) のように思っている理由を日本語で答えなさい。

解答欄

問1		問2		問3	
問4					
問5					

Answers

答えをチェックしましょう。

問1	ever	問2	消防士という仕事	問3	who [that]
問4	they also teach people how to prevent fires				
問5	（今では）人々の手助けをすることはとても重要だとわかっているから。				

問1 現在完了形の重要表現「Have you ever＋動詞の過去分詞形？」（あなたは今までに…したことがありますか）を問う問題。したがって，空所には ever が入ります。

問2 ここでの代名詞 it は前に出た「物・事」を指します。また，it is an exciting and important job（それはワクワクする，重要な仕事である）から，it は何らかの「仕事」であることがわかります。したがって，前に出てきた firefighter（消防士）という仕事が正解になります。

問3 a woman （　　） worked there said to me, … の文には，動詞が2つあります。「1つの文に動詞は1つ」が英語のルールなので，どちらの動詞が文の述語動詞なのかを考えます。a woman （　　） worked のように，「人（___）動詞」の語順に注目すると，空所以下 there までが a woman を修飾していて，空所には worked there と a woman をつなぐ関係代名詞が入ることがわかります。先行詞が「人」で，空所のあとに動詞が続いていることから，who が正解になります（主格の用法）。また，who の代わりに that を使うこともできます。

問4 並べかえは動詞から探しましょう。ここでは，teach と prevent が見つかります。teach は「teach ＋人＋事」（人に事を教える）の語順でよく使われます。また，「how to ＋動詞の原形」（どうやって…すべきか，…する方法）は，ひとカタマリで名詞の働きをします。したがって，they also teach people how to prevent fires の語順になります。

問5 下線部の直前の so（だから）がヒント。so には，「前文＝原因・理由」「後文＝結果」の関係があるので，下線部のように思っている理由は Now I know that helping people is very important. です。理由を答える問題なので，「…だから」のように答えましょう。

重要な表現 9

「tell＋人＋to 不定詞」で「人に…するように言う」

8〜9行目の She told me to go to the Fire Museum in Tokyo.（先生は私に東京にある消防博物館に行くように言った）のように，「tell ＋人＋ to 不定詞」で，「人に…するように言う，すすめる」という意味になります。同じ使い方をする動詞の仲間を確認しておきましょう。

「want ＋人＋ to 不定詞」（人に…してほしい）
「ask ＋人＋ to 不定詞」（人に…するように頼む）

Vocabulary

単語と意味を確認しましょう。

□ ever	[évər]	【副】〈疑問文で〉今までに
□ thought	[θɔ́:t]	【動】think（思う，考える）の過去・過去分詞形
□ think about ～		【熟】～について考える
□ when ...	[hwén]	【接】(…する) ときに
□ ask	[ǽsk]	【動】尋ねる
□ always	[ɔ́:lweiz]	【副】いつも
□ say	[séi]	【動】言う
□ I'd like to ...		【熟】…したいと思う〈I'd＝I would〉
□ exciting	[iksáitiŋ]	【形】興奮させる(ような)，ワクワクする
□ important	[impɔ́:rtənt]	【形】重要な
□ job	[dʒáb]	【名】仕事
□ saw	[sɔ́:]	【動】see (見る) の過去形
□ movie	[mú:vi]	【名】映画
□ how	[háu]	【副】どのようにして
□ people	[pí:pəl]	【名】人々
□ decide	[disáid]	【動】決心する
□ want to ...		【熟】…したいと思う

□ know	[nóu]	【動】知 (ってい) る
□ many	[méni]	【形】多くの
□ thing	[θíŋ]	【名】こと，もの
□ the next day		【熟】次の日
□ teacher	[tí:tʃər]	【名】先生
□ tell ～ to ...		【熟】～に…するように言う
□ museum	[mju(:)zíəm]	【名】博物館，美術館
□ father	[fá:ðər]	【名】父
□ work	[wə́:rk]	【動】働く
□ said	[séd]	【動】say (言う) の過去・過去分詞形
□ of course		【熟】もちろん
□ but ...	[bʌ́t]	【接】しかし…
□ also ...	[ɔ́:lsou]	【副】…もまた
□ teach	[tí:tʃ]	【動】教える
□ how to ...		【熟】…する方法
□ learn	[lə́:rn]	【動】習得する，学ぶ
□ a lot of ～		【熟】多くの～
□ help	[hélp]	【動】手伝う，助ける
□ so ...	[sóu]	【接】だから…

Unit 18

和訳例

　あなたは今までに自分の将来について考えたことがあるだろうか。私がそう聞かれるとき，私はいつも，「私は消防士になりたい」と言う。私にとって，それはワクワクする，重要な仕事なのだ。

　私が10歳だったとき，消防士についての映画を見た。映画の中で彼らが人々をどのように救出するかを見て，私は感動した。私は消防士になりたいと決心した。私は消防士についてたくさんのことを知りたいと思った。

　次の日，先生に消防士について聞いてみた。先生は私に東京にある消防博物館に行くように言った。私が父とその博物館に行くと，そこで働く女性がこう言った。「もちろん消防士は火を消しますが，火事を防ぐ方法を人々に教えたりもするんですよ」と。

　私は映画と消防博物館の女性からたくさんのことを学んだ。今では人々の手助けをすることはとても重要だとわかっている。だから私は消防士になりたい。

Listen & Write!

ディクテーションにチャレンジしましょう！

Have you ever thought about your future? When I am asked, I always say, "I'd (   ) to be a firefighter." For me, it is an exciting and important job.

When I was ten years old, I saw a movie about firefighters.
5 I was (   ) when I saw how they rescued people in the movie. I decided that I wanted to be a firefighter. I wanted to know many things about firefighters.

The (   ) day, I asked my teacher about firefighters. She told me to go to the Fire Museum in Tokyo.
10 When I went to the museum with my father, a woman who worked there said to me, "Of course, firefighters (   ) (   ) fires, but they also teach people how to prevent fires."

I learned a lot of things from the movie and the woman
15 at the museum. Now I know that (   ) people is very important. And so, I want to be a firefighter.

Read aloud!
音読しましょう！

Have you ever / thought about your future? / When I am asked, /
あなたは今までにあるだろうか　　あなたの将来について考えたことが　　私がそう聞かれるとき

I always say, / "I'd like to be / a firefighter." / For me, / it is /
私はいつも言う　　　「私はなりたい　　　　消防士に」　　　私にとって　それは…だ

an exciting and important job. /
ワクワクする，重要な仕事

When I was / ten years old, / I saw a movie / about firefighters. /
私が…だったとき　　　10歳　　　　私は映画を見た　　消防士についての

I was moved / when I saw / how they rescued people / in the movie. /
私は感動した　　私が見たとき　　彼らが人々をどのように救出するかを　　映画の中で

I decided / that I wanted / to be a firefighter. / I wanted / to know /
私は決心した　　　私はしたいと　　消防士になることを　　私はしたいと思った　知ることを

many things / about firefighters. /
たくさんのことを　　消防士について

The next day, / I asked my teacher / about firefighters. /
次の日　　　　　私は先生に聞いた　　　消防士について

She told me / to go to the Fire Museum / in Tokyo. / When I went /
彼女は私に言った　　消防博物館に行くように　　東京にある　　私が行ったとき

to the museum / with my father, / a woman / who worked there /
その博物館に　　　父と一緒に　　　女性が　　そこで働く

said to me, / "Of course, / firefighters / put out fires, /
私に言った　　　「もちろん　　　消防士は　　　　火を消す

but they also teach people / how to prevent fires." /
しかし彼らは人々に教えたりもする　　火事を防ぐ方法を」

I learned / a lot of things / from the movie / and the woman /
私は学んだ　　たくさんのことを　　その映画から　　そしてその女性から

at the museum. / Now I know / that helping people / is very important. /
博物館の　　　今では私はわかっている　　人々の手助けをすることは　　とても重要である

And so, / I want to be / a firefighter.
だから　　私はなりたい　　　消防士に

Listen & Write! (前ページの解答)

Have you ever thought about your future? When I am asked, I always say, "I'd (**like**) to be a firefighter." For me, it is an exciting and important job.

When I was ten years old, I saw a movie about firefighters. I was (**moved**) when I saw how they rescued people in the movie. I decided that I wanted to be a firefighter. I wanted to know many things about firefighters.

The (**next**) day, I asked my teacher about firefighters. She told me to go to the Fire Museum in Tokyo. When I went to the museum with my father, a woman who worked there said to me, "Of course, firefighters (**put**) (**out**) fires, but they also teach people how to prevent fires."

I learned a lot of things from the movie and the woman at the museum. Now I know that (**helping**) people is very important. And so, I want to be a firefighter.

📖 読む時間 目標 **2分51秒**
✏️ 解く時間 **7分**

1回目 _____ 2回目 _____ 3回目 _____

Let's read!

次の英文を読んで，あとの設問に答えなさい。

What is your dream? Some of you want to travel far away from the earth. Maybe we can (1)do this in the 21st century. Some Japanese already went into space. In the future many people will travel in space. We call that future time the age of
5 space travel.

But, before the space age begins, we have to solve (2)one big problem: what will we eat when we travel in space for a long time? Some scientists thought, "If we can grow food in space, we will solve this problem." So they tried to find the
10 best kind of food. Now they have found a good answer— peanuts. Why are peanuts a good food to take into space? There are two reasons for this.

First, we can easily grow peanuts in space, because they can grow in water. Next, (3)peanuts are nutritious. This means
15 peanuts are an important food which have a lot of important things for the body. In the 21st century you may travel in space and eat peanuts.

(栃木県)

(注) space：宇宙　　age：時代　　solve：解決する　　peanuts：ピーナッツ　　easily：容易に

 **Questions**

問1　下線部 (1) の内容を日本語で書きなさい。

問2　下線部 (2) の内容を日本語で書きなさい。

問3　下線部 (3) を和訳しなさい。

問4　本文の見出しとして最も適切なものを選びなさい。
　　　ア．Peanuts will save the earth
　　　イ．Peanuts will be our good friend in the space age
　　　ウ．How to grow peanuts quickly in space
　　　エ．How to improve peanuts in the 21st century

解答欄

問1	
問2	
問3	
問4	

Answers

答えをチェックしましょう。

問1	地球から遠く離れて旅行をする
問2	長期間にわたって宇宙を旅するときに何を食べるかということ。
問3	ピーナッツは栄養価が高い食べ物である。[ピーナッツは栄養豊富である。]
問4	イ	

問1 do this（これをする）は，前に出てきた動詞を含む表現を繰り返すときに用いられます。何を繰り返しているかは，実際にその部分を入れてみるとわかります。ここでは, Maybe we can <u>travel far away from the earth</u> in the 21st century.（おそらく21世紀には<u>地球から遠く離れて旅行をすること</u>ができるだろう）と考えれば意味が通ります。

問2 直後の<u>コロン（:）</u>がヒント。コロンには，直前の内容に<u>説明を加える働き</u>があります。したがって，what will we eat when we travel in space for a long time?（長期間にわたって宇宙を旅するときに何を食べるか）が下線部の内容となります。また，下線部は「問題＝ことがら」ですので，解答の文は「〜ということ」のような終わり方にしましょう。

問3 nutritious という単語の意味がわからなくても，直後の文がヒントになります。This means ...（このことは…を意味します）は，前の文の内容を詳しく説明するときに使います。したがって，下線部は peanuts are an important food which have a lot of important things for the body（ピーナッツは体にとってよいものをたくさん含む重要な食べ物だ）と同じ内容になります。つまり，ここでは「ピーナッツは体にとってよいものをたくさん含む＝栄養価が高い [栄養豊富な] 食べ物である」となります。

問4 見出し（タイトル）は，内容全体を要約するものを選びます。この文の要旨は「宇宙でも簡単に育てることができ，栄養価も高いピーナッツが宇宙時代に適した食べ物である」ことであるため，イが正解と考えられます。アは「宇宙時代」から話がずれており，ウとエは本文には書かれていない内容です。

〈選択肢の和訳〉
　　× ア．ピーナッツは地球を救うだろう
　　○ イ．ピーナッツは宇宙時代には，我々のよき友になるだろう
　　× ウ．どのようにして宇宙で手早くピーナッツを育てるか
　　× エ．どのようにして21世紀にピーナッツを改良するか

Vocabulary

単語と意味を確認しましょう。

☐ dream	[drí:m]	【名】夢
☐ travel	[trǽvəl]	【動】旅行する 【名】旅行
☐ far away from ～		【熟】～から遠く離れて
☐ the earth		【名】地球
☐ maybe	[méibi(:)]	【副】おそらく
☐ in the 21st century		【熟】21世紀に
☐ Japanese	[dʒæpəní:z]	【名】日本人
☐ already	[ɔ:lrédi]	【副】〈肯定文で〉すでに
☐ in the future		【熟】将来
☐ before ...	[bifɔ́:r]	【接】…する前に
☐ begin	[bigín]	【動】始まる
☐ have to ...		【熟】…しなければならない
☐ problem	[prábləm]	【名】問題
☐ for a long time		【熟】長い間,長期間
☐ scientist	[sáiəntist]	【名】科学者
☐ thought	[θɔ́:t]	【動】think (思う,考える)の過去・過去分詞形
☐ grow	[gróu]	【動】栽培する,成長する

☐ food	[fú:d]	【名】食べ物
☐ so ...	[sóu]	【接】そして…
☐ try to ...		【熟】…しようと試みる
☐ find	[fáind]	【動】見つける
☐ best	[bést]	【形】最もよい,最適の
☐ kind	[káind]	【名】種類
☐ answer	[ǽnsər]	【名】答え
☐ why	[hwái]	【副】なぜ
☐ take	[téik]	【動】取る,持っていく
☐ reason	[rí:zən]	【名】理由
☐ first	[fə́:rst]	【副】まず第1に
☐ because ...	[bikɔ́:z]	【接】…なので
☐ water	[wɔ́:tər]	【名】水
☐ next	[nékst]	【副】次に
☐ nutritious	[nju:tríʃəs]	【形】栄養のある
☐ mean	[mí:n]	【動】意味する,…ということである
☐ a lot of ～		【熟】多くの～
☐ important	[impɔ́:rtənt]	【形】重要な,大切な
☐ body	[bádi]	【名】体
☐ may ...	[méi]	【助】…かもしれない

Unit 19

和訳例

　あなたの夢は何だろうか。あなたがたの何人かは地球から遠く離れて旅行したいという人もいるだろう。おそらく21世紀には私たちはこれができるだろう。何人かの日本人はすでに宇宙へ行った。将来は多くの人が宇宙を旅するだろう。私たちは,そうした未来の時代を宇宙旅行時代と呼ぶ。

　しかし,宇宙時代が始まる前に,私たちは1つの大きな問題を解決しなければならない。私たちが長期間にわたって宇宙を旅するときに何を食べるのか,という問題だ。科学者の中には,「宇宙で食べ物を栽培できれば,私たちはこの問題を解決するだろう」と考える人々もいた。そして彼らは最適な食べ物を見つけようとした。今では彼らはよい答えを見つけている。それはピーナッツだ。なぜピーナッツが宇宙へ持っていくのに適した食べ物なのだろうか。これには2つの理由がある。

　まず,ピーナッツは宇宙で容易に栽培できる。なぜならピーナッツは水中で育つことができるからだ。次にピーナッツは栄養価が高い。これはピーナッツが体によいものをたくさん含む重要な食べ物だということだ。21世紀には,あなたは宇宙旅行をしてピーナッツを食べるかもしれない。

Listen & Write!

ディクテーションにチャレンジしましょう！

What is your dream? Some of you want to travel far away from the (   ). Maybe we can do this in the 21st century. Some Japanese already went into space. In the (   ) many people will travel in space. We call
5 that future time the age of space travel.

But, before the space age begins, we have to solve one big (   ): what will we eat when we travel in space for a long time? Some scientists thought, "If we can grow food in space, we will solve this problem." So they tried
10 to find the (   ) kind of food. Now they have found a good answer − peanuts. Why are peanuts a good food to take into space? There are two reasons for this.

First, we can (   ) grow peanuts in space, because they can grow in water. Next, peanuts are nutritious.
15 This means peanuts are an important food which have a lot of good things for the body. In the 21st century you may travel in space and eat peanuts.

Read aloud!

音読しましょう！

What / is your dream? / Some of you / want to travel / far away /
何か　　　　あなたの夢は　　　　あなたがたの何人かは　　　旅行したい　　　　遠く離れて

from the earth. / Maybe / we can do this / in the 21st century. /
地球から　　　　おそらく　　私たちはこれができるだろう　　　21世紀には

Some Japanese / already went into space. / In the future / many people /
何人かの日本人は　　　すでに宇宙へ行った　　　　　将来は　　　　多くの人が

will travel / in space. / We call / that future time / the age of space travel. /
旅するだろう　　宇宙を　　私たちは呼ぶ　そうした未来の時代を　　　宇宙旅行時代と

But, / before the space age / begins, / we have to solve /
しかし　　　宇宙時代が…前に　　　　　始まる　　　私たちは解決しなければならない

one big problem: / what / will we eat / when we travel / in space /
1つの大きな問題を　　　何を　　食べるのか　　私たちが旅するときに　　宇宙を

for a long time? / Some scientists thought, / "If we can grow food /
長期間にわたって　　　科学者の中には考える人もいた　　　「もし私たちが食べ物を栽培できれば

in space, / we will solve / this problem." / So they tried /
宇宙で　　　私たちは解決するだろう　　　この問題を」　　　そして彼らはしようとした

to find the best kind of food. / Now they have found / a good answer /
最適な食べ物を見つけることを　　　今では彼らは見つけている　　　よい答えを

− peanuts. / Why / are peanuts / a good food / to take into space? /
ピーナッツだ　　なぜ　　ピーナッツが　　適した食べ物なのだろう　　　宇宙に持っていくのに

There are / two reasons / for this. /
ある　　　2つの理由が　　　これには

First, / we can easily / grow peanuts / in space, / because they can grow /
まず　　私たちは容易にできる　ピーナッツを栽培する　　宇宙で　　なぜならばピーナッツは育つことができる

in water. / Next, / peanuts are nutritious. / This means / peanuts are /
水中で　　　次に　　　ピーナッツは栄養価が高い　　　これは意味する　　ピーナッツは〜である

an important food / which have / a lot of good things / for the body. /
重要な食べ物　　　　含む　　　たくさんのよいものを　　　　体に

In the 21st century / you may travel / in space / and eat peanuts.
21世紀には　　　あなたは旅行するかもしれない　宇宙を　　そしてピーナッツを食べる

Unit 19

Listen & Write! （前ページの解答）

What is your dream? Some of you want to travel far away from the (　**earth**　). Maybe we can do this in the 21st century. Some Japanese already went into space. In the (　**future**　) many people will travel in space. We call that future time the age of space travel.

But, before the space age begins, we have to solve one big (　**problem**　): what will we eat when we travel in space for a long time? Some scientists thought, "If we can grow food in space, we will solve this problem." So they tried to find the (　**best**　) kind of food. Now they have found a good answer − peanuts. Why are peanuts a good food to take into space? There are two reasons for this.

First, we can (　**easily**　) grow peanuts in space, because they can grow in water. Next, peanuts are nutritious. This means peanuts are an important food which have a lot of good things for the body. In the 21st century you may travel in space and eat peanuts.

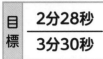

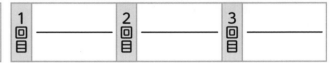

読む時間　目標　2分28秒　1回目　　　　2回目　　　　3回目

解く時間　　　　3分30秒

Let's read!

次の英文を読んで，あとの設問に答えなさい。

Betty : Last fall, I went to Mt. Fuji. The weather was fine, and Mt. Fuji was very beautiful. There are so many beautiful places that I don't want to leave Japan.

Mr. Mori : I'm glad to hear that, but there are some problems, too. Some people leave trash at sightseeing places.

5

Betty : I know. We have the (1) problem in Canada, too. So, at every sightseeing place, we put up a sign that says, "Take only (2), leave only footprints."

Mr. Mori : That's an interesting sign. Does it mean we must not pick any flowers?

10

Betty : Right. And we can only (3) them. When I went to Mt. Tate, people didn't leave any trash there. People were just doing the thing (4)write on our sign. You should be proud of it.

15 Mr. Mori : You're right. We can do it at other sightseeing places, too.

(富山県)

(注) Mt. ～：～山　　leave trash：ごみを残す　　sightseeing：観光
put up a sign：看板を立てる　　footprint：足跡　　pick：つみ取る
be proud of ～：～を誇りに思う

# Questions

問 1 空所 (1) に入れるのに最も適切な語を下のア〜エから選びなさい。

ア．different　　イ．same　　　ウ．other　　　エ．new

問 2 空所 (2) に入れるのに最も適切な語を下のア〜エから選びなさい。

ア．pictures　　イ．animals　　ウ．problems　　エ．flowers

問 3 空所 (3) に入れるのに最も適切な語句を下のア〜エから選びなさい。

ア．look at and get　　　　　イ．walk around and take

ウ．walk around and look at　　エ．come and take

問 4 下線部 (4) の write を適切な形に直しなさい。

Unit 20

解答欄

問1		問2		問3		問4	

Answers

答えをチェックしましょう。

問1	イ	問2	ア	問3	ウ	問4	written

問1 前文に「ごみを残していく人たちがいる」という発言があり，空所のあとの文に「残すのは足跡だけにしよう［ごみを捨てるな］」とあります。ここから，日本の観光地と同じごみ問題を抱えていることがわかるため，イが正解になります。

〈選択肢の和訳〉

　　× ア. 違う　　○ イ. 同じ　　　　× ウ. 他の　　　　× エ. 新しい

問2 空所の前の Take と，続く森先生の発言「それはどんな花もつみ取ってはいけないという意味かな」がヒント。重要表現 take a picture（写真をとる）を使い，Take only pictures（とるのは写真だけにしよう）とすれば，内容にも一致します。したがって，アが正解です。

〈選択肢の和訳〉

　　○ ア. 写真　　× イ. 動物　　　× ウ. 問題　　　　× エ. 花

問3 空所前の1文，Right.（そうです）がヒント。これは前文の「それはどんな花もつみ取ってはいけないという意味かな」に対する発言です。したがって，「見るだけ」という内容になるウが正解です。

〈選択肢の和訳〉

　　× ア. 見て取る　× イ. 歩き回って取る　○ ウ. 歩き回って見る　× エ. やってきて取る

問4 1つの文に述語となる動詞は1つだけ使うのが英語のルールです。この文にはすでに述語動詞 were (just) doing があるので，write を述語ではない形に変えます。問題の write からあとは，直前の名詞 the thing（こと）を説明していると考えられます。名詞を説明するのは形容詞ですから，形容詞の働きをする分詞（動詞の -ing 形や過去分詞形）にします。説明を加える名詞が「している」場合は動詞の -ing 形を，「される」場合は過去分詞形を使います。the thing（こと）は看板に「書かれる」という受け身の関係になるので，過去分詞形の written にします。

重要な表現⓾

形容詞の働きをする分詞

問4で問われている written は，形容詞の働きをする分詞（動詞の -ing 形や過去分詞形）で，名詞のすぐ前や後ろに置かれて名詞を修飾する形容詞の働きをします。使い方のポイントは，説明を加える名詞が「している」場合は動詞の -ing 形を，「される」場合は過去分詞形を使うこと，また分詞の位置については，分詞1語で名詞を修飾するときは名詞の前，「分詞＋語句」という2語以上のカタマリで修飾するときは名詞の後ろに置くことです。

People were just doing <u>the thing</u> <u>written</u> on our sign.
　　　　　　　　　　　　こと　　　　　　看板に書かれた

Vocabulary

単語と意味を確認しましょう。

□ last	[lǽst]	【形】	最後の，この前の
□ fall	[fɔ́:l]	【名】	秋
□ Mt. Fuji		【名】	富士山
□ weather	[wéðər]	【名】	天気
□ fine	[fáin]	【形】	晴れた
□ so ... that ～		【熟】	とても…なので～
□ beautiful	[bjú:təfəl]	【形】	美しい，きれいな
□ want to ...		【熟】	…したいと思う
□ leave	[lí:v]	【動】	去る，置いていく
□ be glad to ...		【熟】	…してうれしく思う
□ hear	[híər]	【動】	聞く
□ some	[sʌ́m]	【形】	いくつかの
□ problem	[prάbləm]	【名】	問題
□ too	[tú:]	【副】	〈肯定文で〉…もまた
□ I know.		【熟】	〈相手に同意して〉そうですね
□ same	[séim]	【形】	同じ

□ Canada	[kǽnədə]	【名】	カナダ
□ so ...	[sóu]	【接】	だから…
□ every	[évri]	【形】	あらゆる，どの…も
□ say	[séi]	【動】	(掲示板などに)書いてある
□ take a picture		【熟】	写真をとる
□ interesting	[íntərəstiŋ]	【形】	おもしろい
□ mean	[mí:n]	【動】	意味する
□ must not ...		【助】	…してはいけない
□ flower	[fláuər]	【名】	花
□ right	[ráit]	【形】	正しい，〈返答として〉そのとおり
□ walk around		【熟】	歩き回る
□ look at ～		【熟】	～を見る
□ Mt. Tate		【名】	立山
□ just	[dʒʌ́st]	【副】	まさに
□ written	[rítən]	【動】	write (書く)の過去分詞形
□ should ...	[ʃúd]	【助】	…すべきである

和訳例

Betty：昨年の秋，私は富士山へ行きました。天気がよくて，富士山はとてもきれいでした。とてもたくさんの美しい場所があるので，日本を離れたくありません。

Mr. Mori：それを聞いてうれしいけど，いくつか問題もあるんだ。観光地にごみを残していく人たちがいるんだ。

Betty：そうですね。カナダもまた同じ問題を抱えています。だからどの観光地にも，「とるのは写真だけにしよう，残すのは足跡だけにしよう」と書いた看板を立てています。

Mr. Mori：それはおもしろい看板だね。それはどんな花もつみ取ってはいけないという意味かな。

Betty：そうです。私たちは歩き回って花を見ることだけができます。私が立山（注：富山県にある飛騨山脈系の山）に行ったとき，みんなそこに何のごみも残しませんでした。みんな，まさにカナダの看板に書かれていることを実行していたのです。あなたは，そのことを誇りに思うべきです。

Mr. Mori：そうだね。私たちは他の観光地でもそうすることができるね。

Unit 20

Listen & Write!

ディクテーションにチャレンジしましょう！

Betty : Last fall, I went to Mt. Fuji. The weather was fine, and Mt. Fuji was very beautiful. There are so many beautiful places that I don't want to leave Japan.

Mr. Mori : I'm (　　　　　　　) to hear that, but there are
5　some problems, too. Some people leave trash at sightseeing places.

Betty : I know. We have the same problem in Canada, too. So, at every sightseeing place, we put up a sign that says, "(　　　　　) only pictures, (　　　　　)
10　only footprints."

Mr. Mori : That's an interesting sign. Does it mean we (　　　　　　) not pick any flowers?

Betty : Right. And we can only walk around and look at them. When I went to Mt. Tate, people didn't leave any
15　trash there. People were just doing the thing written on our sign. You (　　　　　　) be proud of it.

Mr. Mori : You're right. We can do it at other sightseeing places, too.

Read aloud!
音読しましょう！

Betty : Last fall, / I went / to Mt. Fuji. / The weather was fine, /
昨年の秋　　　私は行きました　　富士山へ　　　　天気がよかった

and Mt. Fuji / was very beautiful. / There are / so many
そして富士山は　　　とてもきれいでした　　　　ある　　とてもたくさんの

beautiful places / that I don't want / to leave Japan. /
美しい場所が　　　だから私は望まない　　　日本を離れることを

Mr. Mori : I'm glad / to hear that, / but there are / some problems, /
私はうれしい　　それを聞いて　　　しかし，ある　　　いくつか問題が

too. / Some people / leave trash / at sightseeing places. /
もまた　　何人かの人たちは　　ごみを残す　　　観光地に

Betty : I know. / We have the same problem / in Canada, / too. / So, /
そうですね　　私たちは同じ問題を抱えています　　カナダで　　もまた　　だから

at every sightseeing place, / we put up a sign / that says, /
どの観光地にも　　　私たちは看板を立てています　　と書いてある

"Take only pictures, / leave only footprints." /
「写真だけとろう　　　足跡だけ残そう」

Mr. Mori : That's an interesting sign. / Does it mean / we must not pick /
それはおもしろい看板だね　　それは意味しますか　　私たちはつみ取ってはいけない

any flowers? /
どんな花も

Betty : Right. / And we can / only walk around / and look at them. /
そうです　そして私たちはできます　歩き回ることだけ　　そしてそれらを見ること

When I went / to Mt. Tate, / people didn't leave /
私が行ったとき　　　立山に　　　　　人々は残しませんでした

any trash / there. / People / were just doing the thing /
何のごみも　　そこに　　人々は　　まさにそのことを実行していました

written on our sign. / You should / be proud of it. /
私たちの看板に書かれている　　あなたはすべきです　そのことを誇りに思う

Mr. Mori : You're right. / We can do it / at other sightseeing places, /
そうだね　　私たちはそうすることができる　　　他の観光地で

too.
もまた

Unit 20

Listen & Write! （前ページの解答）

Betty : Last fall, I went to Mt. Fuji. The weather was fine, and Mt. Fuji was very beautiful. There are so many beautiful places that I don't want to leave Japan.

Mr. Mori : I'm (**glad**) to hear that, but there are some problems, too. Some people leave trash at sightseeing places.

Betty : I know. We have the same problem in Canada, too. So, at every sightseeing place, we put up a sign that says, "(**Take**) only pictures, (**leave**) only footprints."

Mr. Mori : That's an interesting sign. Does it mean we (**must**) not pick any flowers?

Betty : Right. And we can only walk around and look at them. When I went to Mt. Tate, people didn't leave any trash there. People were just doing the thing written on our sign. You (**should**) be proud of it.

Mr. Mori : You're right. We can do it at other sightseeing places, too.

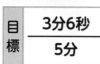

Let's read!

次の英文を読んで，あとの設問に答えなさい。

Do you know how (1) your school's swimming pool is? If you don't, you can jump into the pool and measure the depth of it. Then, how do you measure the depth of a lake or an ocean? People in the old days measured it by dropping a rope
5 with a stone on it into the water.

Today, we are able to know the depth of the ocean with an echo sounder. An echo sounder on a ship sends out a sound. The sound travels through the water at about 1.6 km a second. It hits the ocean floor and comes back to the echo
10 sounder on the ship a few seconds later. The echo sounder puts dark marks on paper. By reading the marks, we measure the time and know how deep the ocean is.

The echo sounder does much more than this. It keeps sending out sounds as the ship moves. If the ship passes over
15 a mountain in the ocean, the echo sounder shows us the shape of the mountain. In this way we can know about the ocean floor under the ship.

(国立高専 改)

(注) measure：測定する　　depth：深さ　　rope：ロープ　　echo sounder：音波探知器
　　second：秒　　mark：しるし　　deep：深い　　shape：形

 **Questions**

問1 空所（1）に入れるのに最も適切な語を書きなさい。

問2 本文の内容に合うように，下の英文の空所に最も適切な語を書きなさい。ただし2については数字で答えなさい。

1. What did the people in the old days use to know the depth of the water?

   They used a (　　) and a (　　).

2. How deep is the water when a sound reaches the ocean floor and returns to the ship in 4 seconds?

   The water is about (　　) km deep.

3. What does an echo sounder put on paper?

   It puts (　　)(　　).

4. What does an echo sounder show us?

   It shows us the (　　) of the ocean and the (　　) of its floor.

Unit 21

解答欄

問1			
問2	1		2
	3		4

Answers

答えをチェックしましょう。

問1		deep		
問2	1	rope, stone [stone, rope]	2	3.2
	3	dark, marks	4	depth, shape

問1 この文のすぐあとに続く文がヒント。「もし知らなければプールに飛び込んでその depth（深さ）を測ることができる」とあることから，「どのくらい深いですか」と尋ねるとよいことがわかります。「どのくらいの…？」と how を使って尋ねるときは，how long（どのくらいの長さ）のように，「how ＋形容詞［副詞］…?」という形で使うのが基本です。したがって，形容詞の deep（深い）を入れます。depth（深さ）は名詞です。

問2 1. 4〜5行目に「昔の人々は石を付けたロープを水中に投げ入れて，深さを測定した」とあります。したがって，rope（ロープ）と stone（石）が正解だとわかります。

〈問題文の和訳〉 「昔の人々が水の深さを知るために使ったものは何ですか」
「彼らはロープと石［石とロープ］を使いました」

2. 8〜9行目に「音は毎秒約 1.6km の速さで水中を伝わる」とあります。したがって，船と海底の往復の距離「1.6(km) × 4(秒) = 6.4km」の半分の 3.2km が海の深さとなります。

〈問題文の和訳〉 「音が4秒で海の底に到達し船に戻ってくるとき，水はどのくらいの深さですか」
「水は約 3.2km の深さです」

3. 10 〜 11 行目に「音波探知器は紙の上に dark marks（黒い印）を付ける」とあります。したがって，dark marks が正解です。

〈問題文の和訳〉 「音波探知器が紙の上に付けるのは何ですか」
「それは黒い印を付けます」

4. 6〜7行目に「音波探知器を使って海の the depth（深さ）を知ることができる」，15 〜 16 行目に「音波探知器が（海の中の）山の the shape（形）を教えてくれる」とあります。したがって，最初の空所には depth が，あとの空所には shape が入ります。空所はどちらも the のあとなので名詞が入ります。最初の空所に形容詞の deep（深い）を入れないように注意しましょう。

〈問題文の和訳〉 「音波探知器は私たちに何を示しますか」
「それは私たちに海の深さと海の底の形を示してくれます」

Vocabulary

単語と意味を確認しましょう。

□ how	[háu]	【副】	どれくらい
□ deep	[díːp]	【形】	深い
□ swimming pool		【名】	(水泳用の) プール
□ if ...	[if]	【接】	もし…ならば
□ jump	[dʒʌ́mp]	【動】	跳ぶ
□ then	[ðén]	【副】	では
□ lake	[léik]	【名】	湖
□ ocean	[óuʃən]	【名】	海
□ in the old days		【熟】	昔に [の]
□ stone	[stóun]	【名】	石
□ today	[tədéi]	【副】	今では, この頃は
□ be able to ...		【熟】	…できる
□ ship	[ʃíp]	【名】	船
□ send out		【熟】	送り出す, 放つ
□ sound	[sáund]	【名】	音
□ travel	[trǽvəl]	【動】	〈光・音などが〉伝わる
□ through ~	[θrúː]	【前】	~を通って

□ hit	[hít]	【動】	打つ, ぶつかる
□ ocean floor		【名】	海底
□ come back to ~		【熟】	~へ戻る
□ a few		【熟】	2~3の, 少しの
□ later	[léitər]	【副】	あとで
□ put a mark on ~		【熟】	~に印を付ける
□ dark	[dáːrk]	【形】	暗い, 黒い
□ paper	[péipər]	【名】	紙
□ much	[mʌ́tʃ]	【副】	〈比較級を強調して〉 ずっと
□ more	[mɔ́ːr]	【名】	それ以上 [より多く] のこと
□ keep -ing		【熟】	…し続ける
□ as ...	[əz]	【接】	…(する) とき, につれて
□ move	[múːv]	【動】	動く
□ pass over ~		【熟】	~の上を通り過ぎる
□ show	[ʃóu]	【動】	見せる, 示す
□ in this way		【熟】	このようにして
□ under ~	[ʌ́ndər]	【前】	~の下の [に]

Unit 21

和訳例

　あなたは自分の学校のプールがどのくらい深いか知っているだろうか。もしあなたが知らなければ，プールに飛び込んでその深さを測ることができる。では，あなたは湖や海の深さはどうやって測定するだろうか。昔の人々は，石を付けたロープを水中に投げ入れて，深さを測定した。

　今では，私たちは音波探知器を使って海の深さを知ることができる。船上の音波探知器が音を発信する。その音は毎秒約 1.6km の速さで水中を伝わる。音は海の底にぶつかり，数秒後に船上の音波探知器に戻ってくる。音波探知器は紙の上に黒い印を付ける。その印を読むことによって，私たちは時間を測定し，海がどのくらい深いかがわかる。

　音波探知器は，さらにこれよりずっと多くのことをする。それは船が動くとき，音を発信し続ける。もし船が海の中にある山の上を通り過ぎたら，音波探知器がその山の形を私たちに示してくれる。このようにして私たちは船の下の海底について知ることができる。

Listen & Write!

ディクテーションにチャレンジしましょう！

Do you know how deep your school's swimming pool is? If you don't, you can jump into the pool and measure the depth of it. Then, how do you measure the depth of a lake or an ocean? People in the old days measured it by

5 (   ) a rope with a stone on it into the water.

Today, we are able to know the depth of the ocean with an echo sounder. An echo sounder on a ship sends out a sound. The sound travels (   ) the

10 water at about 1.6 km a second. It hits the ocean floor and comes back to the echo sounder on the ship a few seconds (   ). The echo sounder puts dark marks on paper. By reading the marks, we measure the time and know how deep the ocean is.

15   The echo sounder does much (   ) than this. It keeps sending out sounds as the ship moves. If the ship passes over a mountain in the ocean, the echo sounder shows us the (   ) of the mountain. In this way we can know about the ocean floor under the ship.

Read aloud!
音読しましょう！

Do you know / how deep / your school's swimming pool is? / If you don't, /
あなたは知ってるだろうか　どのくらい深いかを　　　　自分の学校のプールが　　　　もしあなたが知らなければ

you can jump / into the pool / and measure / the depth of it. / Then, / how /
あなたは跳べる　　　プールの中に　　そして測る　　　その深さを　　では　　どうやって

do you measure / the depth / of a lake or an ocean? / People / in the old days /
あなたは測定するだろうか　深さを　　　湖や海の　　　　人々は　　　昔の

measured it / by dropping a rope / with a stone on it / into the water. /
それを測定した　ロープを投げ入れることによって　それに石を付けた　　　水中に

Today, / we are able to know / the depth / of the ocean / with an echo
今では　　　私たちは知ることができる　　　深さを　　　海の　　　音波探知器を使って

sounder. / An echo sounder / on a ship / sends out a sound. / The sound travels /
音波探知器が　　　船上の　　　音を発信する　　　　その音は伝わる

through the water / at about 1.6 km / a second. / It hits the ocean floor / and
水中を　　　　　約1.6kmで　　　毎秒　　　それは海の底にぶつかる

comes back / to the echo sounder / on the ship / a few seconds later. / The echo
そして戻ってくる　　　音波探知器に　　　船上の　　　数秒後に　　　音波探知器は

sounder / puts dark marks / on paper. / By reading the marks, / we measure the
黒い印を付ける　　　紙の上に　　その印を読むことによって　　私たちは時間を測定する

time / and know / how deep / the ocean is. /
そしてわかる　どのくらい深いかが　　海が

The echo sounder does / much more than this. / It keeps sending out sounds /
音波探知器はする　　さらにこれよりずっと多くのことを　　　それは音を発信し続ける

as the ship moves. / If the ship / passes over a mountain / in the ocean, /
船が動くとき　　　もし船が　　　山の上を通り過ぎたら　　　海の中にある

the echo sounder / shows us / the shape / of the mountain. / In this way /
音波探知器が　　私たちに示してくれる　　形を　　　その山の　　　このようにして

we can know / about the ocean floor / under the ship.
私たちは知ることができる　　　海底について　　　　　船の下の

Unit 21

📖 読む時間 　目標　2分32秒
✏️ 解く時間 　　　6分

1回目 ―
2回目 ―
3回目 ―

Let's read!

次の文章は，北アメリカの先住民（Native Americans）について述べたものです。これを読んで，あとの設問に答えなさい。

　　Long, long ago, people came to America. The first Americans lived in big groups. There were a lot of different groups all over the country. Each of the groups had its own language, its own way （ 1 ） life and its own name. When
5 Columbus arrived （ 2 ） America （ 3 ） 1492, he thought he was in India. So (these, he, "Indians", people, called).

　　Some groups, （ 4 ） example, lived along the sea. They fished, and much of their food came （ 5 ） the sea. Other groups lived in the hot desert. They were farmers. Some
10 other groups hunted bison. Bison are always moving, so the groups had to move, too.

　　Today, more than thirty percent of all Native Americans live on reservations. The others live in cities and towns. Many Native Americans say they "walk in two worlds." They are
15 part of today's America, but they also keep the ways of their people − the first Americans.

(岩手県)

（注）way：仕方，方法　　Columbus：コロンブス（15〜16世紀のイタリア生まれの航海家）
　　　desert：砂漠　　bison：アメリカ野牛，バイソン　　Native American：アメリカ先住民
　　　reservations：アメリカ先住民のために特別に定められた居住地

Questions

問1 空所 (1) ～ (5) に入れるのに最も適切な前置詞を書きなさい。

問2 下線部を意味の通る英文になるように並べかえなさい。

問3 本文の内容について，次の問いに英語で答えなさい。
1. Why did the groups that hunted bison have to move?
2. What percent of Native Americans live in cities and towns?

解答欄

問1	(1)		(2)		(3)	
	(4)		(5)			
問2						
問3	1					
	2					

Answers

答えをチェックしましょう。

問1	(1)	of	(2)	in	(3)	in
	(4)	for	(5)	from		

問2		he called these people "Indians"

問3	1	Because bison are [were] always moving.
	2	About[Less than] seventy percent of them live there. [About seventy percent. / Less than seventy percent.]

問1 (1) a way <u>of</u> life（生活様式）　　(2) arrive <u>in</u> ～（～に到着する）
(3)「<u>in</u>＋年号」（～年に）　　(4) <u>for</u> example（例えば）
(5) come <u>from</u> ～（～から生じる，～に由来する）
(2) の arrive <u>in</u> ～は，国や町のような広い範囲の場所に到着するときに使い，arrive <u>at</u> ～は，建物などに到着するときに使います。

問2 重要表現 call A B（A を B と呼ぶ）を問う問題です。与えられている単語の中で，代名詞 he は主語にしかなれないので，これが主語になります。あとは意味を考え，A と B を決定すれば完成です。なお，並べかえ問題のため，ピリオドが最後に付いていますが，ピリオドやカンマはクォーテーション・マーク（" "）の内側に入れるのが基本です。したがって，英作文では he called these people "Indians.<u>"</u> のように書くようにしましょう。

問3 1. 10 ～ 11 行目にヒントがあります。「文1＋<u>so</u>＋文2」には「文1，だから文2」という意味で，「文1」が原因・理由を，「文2」がその結果を表します。したがって，「移動しなければならない理由」は「文1」にあることになります。ただし，Why …? という質問には，Because（…だから）や to 不定詞（…するため）などの表現で答える点に注意しましょう。ここでは bison の習性を述べるので，時制は現在進行形にしますが were を使っても正解です。
〈問題文の和訳〉「アメリカ野牛を狩猟していた集団が移動しなければならなかったのはなぜですか」

2. 12 ～ 13 行目がヒント。「30％以上が特別居住地に住んでいる。その他の人々は都市や町に住んでいる」とあるので，about seventy percent（約 70％）や less than seventy percent（70％未満）などの表現を使って答えます。代名詞などに直せるものは直して答えるのがポイントになります。
〈問題文の和訳〉「アメリカ先住民の何％が都市や町に住んでいますか」

Vocabulary

単語と意味を確認しましょう。

☐ long, long ago		【熟】	遠い昔
☐ people	[píːpəl]	【名】	人々, 民族
☐ came	[kéim]	【動】	come (来る) の過去形
☐ America	[əmérikə]	【名】	アメリカ
☐ American	[əmérikən]	【名】	アメリカ人
☐ group	[grúːp]	【名】	グループ, 集団
☐ in big groups		【熟】	大きな集団で
☐ different	[dífərənt]	【形】	異なった
☐ all over the country		【熟】	国中に
☐ each	[íːtʃ]	【代】	それぞれ
☐ own	[óun]	【形】	自分自身の
☐ language	[læŋgwidʒ]	【名】	言語, 言葉
☐ way of life		【名】	生活様式
☐ arrive	[əráiv]	【動】	着く
☐ thought	[θɔ́ːt]	【動】	think (思う, 考える) の過去・過去分詞形
☐ India	[índiə]	【名】	インド
☐ so ...	[sóu]	【接】	だから…
☐ Indian	[índiən]	【名】	インド人

☐ some -s ... other -s ...		【熟】	…な〜もあれ ば, …な〜も ある
☐ for example		【熟】	例えば
☐ along 〜	[əlɔ́(ː)ŋ]	【前】	〜に沿って
☐ fish	[fíʃ]	【動】	魚を捕る
☐ much of 〜		【熟】	〜の多く
☐ come from 〜		【熟】	〜から生じる
☐ hot	[hát]	【形】	暑い, 熱い
☐ farmer	[fáːrmər]	【名】	農民
☐ hunt	[hʌ́nt]	【動】	狩猟する
☐ move	[múːv]	【動】	動く, 移動する
☐ have to ...		【熟】	…しなければ ならない
☐ more than 〜		【熟】	〜より多く, 〜以上
☐ thirty	[θə́ːrti]	【形】	30 の
☐ world	[wə́ːrld]	【名】	世界
☐ part of 〜		【熟】	〜の一部 (分)
☐ also ...	[ɔ́ːlsou]	【副】	…もまた
☐ keep	[kíːp]	【動】	保つ, 続ける

Unit 22

和訳例

　遠い昔，人々がアメリカ（大陸）にやってきた。最初のアメリカ人は大きな集団で生活していた。国中にたくさんの異なる集団があった。それぞれの集団は，自分たちの言語を持ち，自分たちの生活様式と名前を持っていた。1492 年にコロンブスがアメリカに着いたとき，彼は自分がインドにいるのだと思った。そのため，彼はこうした人々を「インディアン」と呼んだ。

　例えば，海沿いに住む集団がいた。彼らは魚を捕り，そして彼らの食べ物の多くは海から得たものだった。暑い砂漠に住む他の集団もいた。彼らは農民だった。また別の集団はアメリカ野牛の狩りをしていた。アメリカ野牛はいつも移動しているので，その集団も移動しなければならなかった。

　今では，全アメリカ先住民の 30% 以上が特別居住地に住んでいる。その他の人々は都市や町に住んでいる。多くのアメリカ先住民が，自分たちは「2 つの世界を歩んでいる」という。彼らは今のアメリカの一部だが，また最初のアメリカ人としての自分たちの民族のやり方を続けているのだ。

Listen & Write!

ディクテーションにチャレンジしましょう！

Long, long ago, people came to America. The first Americans lived in big (   ). There were a lot of different groups all over the country. Each of the groups had its own language, its own way of life and its own

5 name. When Columbus (   ) in America in 1492, he thought he was in India. So he called these people "Indians."

Some groups, for example, lived along the sea. They fished, and much of their food came from the sea. Other

10 groups lived in the hot desert. They were farmers. Some other groups hunted bison. Bison are always moving, so the groups (   ) (   ) move, too.

Today, more than thirty (   ) of all Native Americans live on reservations. The others live in cities

15 and towns. Many Native Americans say they "walk in two worlds." They are (   ) of today's America, but they also keep the ways of their people —— the first Americans.

Read aloud!

音読しましょう！

Long, long ago, / people came / to America. / The first Americans /
遠い昔　　　　　　人々がやってきた　　　アメリカに　　　　　最初のアメリカ人は

lived / in big groups. / There were / a lot of different groups / all over
生活していた　大きな集団で　　　あった　　　たくさんの異なる集団が　　　　国中に

the country. / Each of the groups / had its own language, / its own way
それぞれの集団は　　　　自分たちの言語を持っていた　　　自分たちの生活様式を

of life / and its own name. / When Columbus / arrived in America / in 1492, /
そして自分たちの名前を　　　コロンブスが…とき　　　アメリカに着いた　　　1492年に

he thought / he was in India. / So he called these people / "Indians." /
彼は思った　　彼はインドにいるのだと　　　だから，彼はこうした人々を呼んだ　　「インディアン」と

Some groups, / for example, / lived along the sea. / They fished, /
いくつかの集団が　　　　例えば　　　　海沿いに住んでいた　　　彼らは魚を捕った

and much of their food / came from the sea. / Other groups / lived in
そして彼らの食べ物の多くは　　　海から得たものだった　　　他の集団は　　　暑い砂漠に住んでいた

the hot desert. / They were farmers. / Some other groups / hunted bison. /
彼らは農民だった　　　　　また別の集団は　　　　アメリカ野牛の狩りをしていた

Bison are always moving, / so the groups / had to move, / too. /
アメリカ野牛はいつも移動している　　だからその集団は　　移動しなければならなかった　もまた

Today, / more than thirty percent / of all Native Americans /
今では　　　　　30%以上が　　　　　　　全アメリカ先住民の

live on reservations. / The others / live in cities / and towns. /
特別居住地に住んでいる　　　その他の人々は　　都市に住んでいる　　　そして町に

Many Native Americans say / they "walk / in two worlds." / They are /
多くのアメリカ先住民が言う　　自分たちは「歩んでいる　　2つの世界を」　　彼らは…である

part of today's America, / but they also / keep the ways / of their people /
今のアメリカの一部　　　　だが彼らはまた　　やり方を続けている　　自分たちの民族の

— the first Americans.
つまり最初のアメリカ人の

Unit 22

Listen & Write! （前ページの解答）

Long, long ago, people came to America. The first Americans lived in big (**groups**). There were a lot of different groups all over the country. Each of the groups had its own language, its own way of life and its own name. When Columbus (**arrived**) in America in 1492, he thought he was in India. So he called these people "Indians."

Some groups, for example, lived along the sea. They fished, and much of their food came from the sea. Other groups lived in the hot desert. They were farmers. Some other groups hunted bison. Bison are always moving, so the groups (**had**) (**to**) move, too.

Today, more than thirty (**percent**) of all Native Americans live on reservations. The others live in cities and towns. Many Native Americans say they "walk in two worlds." They are (**part**) of today's America, but they also keep the ways of their people — the first Americans.

Unit 23

英文の長さ **192** words

|50|100|150|200|

読む時間 | 目標 | 3分12秒
解く時間 | | 4分

1回目 ——— 2回目 ——— 3回目 ———

Let's read!

次の英文を読んで，あとの設問に答えなさい。

"Season" is a very important word to Japanese people. They often use this word when they talk about food. They think (1). They call it "*shun*" in Japanese. For example, many bamboo shoots grow in spring. Japanese people can get
5 a lot of good new bamboo shoots at this time. So, they think spring is the best season for this food.

Today, it is not easy for Japanese people to feel the sense of "*shun*," because there are many kinds of food they can get in all four seasons. Spinach is one of these kinds of
10 food. There are not many people who know winter is the best season for spinach, (2).

Many Japanese people still want to feel the sense of "*shun*." There are two reasons for this. First, it is easier to get good food in its best season. For example, they don't need
15 much money to buy good spinach in winter. Second, they can get a sense of the season. Just like some birds and flowers, bamboo shoots can tell Japanese people that spring has come.

(栃木県)

(注) *shun*: 旬（しゅん）　bamboo shoots：タケノコ　spinach：ホウレンソウ
reasons：理由　a sense of the season：季節感

 **Questions**

問1 空所 (1)，(2) に入れるのに最も適切なものを，下のア～エからそれぞれ選びなさい。

(1) ア．they have four seasons in Japan
   イ．each Japanese food has its own name
   ウ．Japanese people love the four seasons very much
   エ．each Japanese food has its best season

(2) ア．because people can get spinach in other seasons
   イ．because people can get many kinds of food
   ウ．because people can tell the best season of each food
   エ．because people can buy good spinach only in winter

問2 第3段落の内容を要約すると次のようになります。空所 A，B に，それぞれふさわしい日本語を書きなさい。

「日本人の多くが，（　A　）と今も考えている。その理由の1つは（　B　）であり，そしてもう1つは，季節を感じることができるからである」

Unit 23

解答欄

問1	(1)		(2)	
問2	A			
	B			

141

Answers

答えをチェックしましょう。

問1	(1)		エ	(2)		ア
問2	A	旬を感じたい				
	B	品質のよい食べ物が簡単に〔安く〕手に入るから				

問1　(1) They think (　　). They call <u>it</u> "*shun*" in Japanese. は,「日本人は (　　　)
と考えている。日本人は日本語でそれを『旬』と呼ぶ」という意味なので, 空所
には空所のあとの it が指す内容＝「旬」が入るとわかります。旬とは, 個々の
食べ物が最もおいしく食べられる季節のことなので, エが正解になります。また,
旬の意味を知らない場合でも, 続く For example 以降の文から, 旬の意味が推
測できます。なお, call it "*shun*" は重要表現 call A B(A を B と呼ぶ) です。
この表現では, A と B の間に A=B の関係があることを覚えておくと便利です。

　〈選択肢の和訳〉
　　× ア. 日本には四季がある
　　× イ. 日本の食べ物1つ1つが個々の名前を持っている
　　× ウ. 日本人は四季が大好きだ
　　○ エ. 日本のどの食べ物にも最適な季節がある

　(2) 空所を含む文 There are not many people who know winter is the best
season for spinach, (　　). は,「冬がホウレンソウにとって最適な季節だと
知っている人は多くない, (　　　)」という意味です。この部分は第2段落の最
後の文で, 空所は第2段落の内容全体がヒントになります。この段落は「今では
四季を通してさまざまな食べ物が手に入るので, 日本人が旬を知るのは簡単では
ない」という趣旨で, その例としてホウレンソウを挙げているので, 同じ内容に
なるアが正解です。

　〈選択肢の和訳〉
　　○ ア. 他の季節でもホウレンソウを手に入れることができるので
　　× イ. 多くの種類の食べ物を手に入れることができるので
　　× ウ. 食べ物1つ1つの最適な季節を見分けることができるので
　　× エ. 冬にだけ, おいしいホウレンソウを買うことができるので

問2　(A) 12〜13行目に「多くの日本人が, それでも『旬』の感覚を感じたがっている」
とあるので,「旬を感じたい」という内容を書けば正解です。
　(B) 13〜14行目に「第1に, 食べ物にとって最適な季節には, 品質のよい食べ物
を手に入れることがより簡単だからだ」とあるので, その内容を書けば正解です。
ただし, ここは「理由の1つは」が主語なので,「…だから」のように答えましょう。

Vocabulary

単語と意味を確認しましょう。

□ season	[síːzən]	【名】	季節
□ important	[impɔ́ːrtənt]	【形】	重要な, 大切な
□ word	[wə́ːrd]	【名】	単語, 言葉
□ Japanese	[dʒæpəníːz]	【形】	日本の
□ talk about ～		【熟】	～について話す
□ think	[θíŋk]	【動】	思う, 考える
□ each	[íːtʃ]	【形】	それぞれの, どの～も
□ best	[bést]	【形】	最もよい, 最適の
□ call A B		【熟】	AをBと呼ぶ
□ in Japanese		【熟】	日本語で
□ for example		【熟】	例えば
□ many	[méni]	【形】	多くの
□ grow	[gróu]	【動】	成長する, 育つ
□ spring	[spríŋ]	【名】	春
□ get	[gét]	【動】	得る
□ so ...	[sóu]	【接】	だから…
□ easy	[íːzi]	【形】	容易な, 簡単な
□ feel	[fíːl]	【動】	感じる

□ sense	[séns]	【名】	感覚
□ because ...	[bikɔ́ːz]	【接】	なぜなら…だから
□ kind	[káind]	【名】	種類
□ winter	[wíntər]	【名】	冬
□ other	[ʌ́ðər]	【形】	他の
□ still	[stíl]	【副】	それでもなお
□ want to ...		【熟】	…したい
□ first	[fə́ːrst]	【副】	まず第1に, 1番目に
□ easier	[íːziər]	【形】	easy (容易な) の比較級
□ need	[níːd]	【動】	必要とする
□ much	[mʌ́tʃ]	【形】	多くの
□ money	[mʌ́ni]	【名】	金
□ second	[sékənd]	【副】	第2に, 2番目に
□ like ～	[láik]	【前】	～のように
□ bird	[bə́ːrd]	【名】	鳥
□ flower	[fláuər]	【名】	花
□ tell	[tél]	【動】	伝える, 教える

―― 和訳例 ――

　「季節」は日本人にとって，とても大切な言葉だ。日本人は食べ物について話すとき，よくこの言葉を使う。日本人は日本のどの食べ物にも最適な季節があると考えている。日本人は日本語でそれを「旬」と呼ぶ。例えば，春にはたくさんのタケノコが育つ。日本人はこの時期にたくさんのおいしくて新鮮なタケノコを手に入れることができる。だから，日本人は春がタケノコに最適な季節だと考えるのだ。

　今では，日本人が「旬」の感覚を感じるのは簡単なことではない，なぜなら四季を通して手に入れることができる多くの種類の食べ物があるからだ。ホウレンソウは，そうした食べ物の1つだ。冬がホウレンソウにとって最適な季節だと知っている人は多くない。なぜならホウレンソウは他の季節でも手に入れることができるからだ。

　多くの日本人が，それでも「旬」の感覚を感じたがっている。これには2つの理由がある。第1に，食べ物にとって最適な季節には，品質のよい食べ物を手に入れることがより簡単だからだ。例えば，冬においしいホウレンソウを買うためにお金はあまり必要ではない。第2に，季節感を得ることができる。ちょうど鳥や花のように，タケノコは日本人に春が来たことを教えてくれる。

Unit 23

Listen & Write!

ディクテーションにチャレンジしましょう！

"Season" is a very important word to Japanese people. They (   ) use this word when they talk about food. They think each Japanese food has its (   ) season. They call it "*shun*" in Japanese. For example, many
5 bamboo shoots grow in spring. Japanese people can get a lot of good new bamboo shoots at this time. So, they think spring is the best season for this food.

Today, it is not easy for Japanese people to (   ) the sense of "*shun*," because there are many kinds of food
10 they can get in all four seasons. Spinach is one of these kinds of food. There are not many people who know winter is the best season for spinach, because people can get spinach in other seasons.

Many Japanese people still want to feel the sense of
15 "*shun*." There are two reasons for this. First, it is easier to get good food in its best season. For example, they don't (   ) much money to buy good spinach in winter. Second, they can get a sense of the season. Just like some birds and flowers, bamboo shoots can tell Japanese people
20 that spring (   ) come.

Read aloud!

音読しましょう！

"Season" is / a very important word / to Japanese people. /
「季節」は　　　　　　　　　とても大切な言葉だ　　　　　　　日本人にとって

They often use this word / when they talk / about food. / They think /
彼らはよくこの言葉を使う　　　　　彼らが話すとき　　　食べ物について　　　彼らは考えている

each Japanese food / has its best season. / They call it / "shun" /
日本のどの食べ物にも　　　　最適な季節がある　　　　彼らはそれを呼ぶ　　「旬」と

in Japanese. / For example, / many bamboo shoots / grow in spring. /
日本語で　　　　　　例えば　　　　たくさんのタケノコが　　　　　　春に育つ

Japanese people can get / a lot of good new bamboo shoots /
日本人は手に入れることができる　　　　たくさんのおいしくて新鮮なタケノコを

at this time. / So, / they think / spring is the best season / for this food. /
この時期に　　　だから　　彼らは考える　　春が最適な季節であると　　　　この食べ物に

Today, / it is not easy / for Japanese people / to feel the sense of
今では　　　簡単なことではない　　　日本人にとって　　　　「旬」の感覚を感じるのは

"shun," / because there are / many kinds of food / they can get / in all four
　　　　　なぜならあるからだ　　　多くの種類の食べ物が　　彼らが手に入れることができる　　四季を通して

seasons. / Spinach is / one of these kinds of food. / There are not /
　　　　ホウレンソウは　　　そうした食べ物の１つだ　　　　　いない

many people / who know / winter is the best season / for spinach, /
多くの人は　　　　知っている　　　　冬が最適な季節だと　　　　ホウレンソウにとって

because people / can get spinach / in other seasons. /
なぜなら人々は…からだ　ホウレンソウを手に入れることができる　　　他の季節に

Many Japanese people / still want to feel / the sense of "shun." /
多くの日本人が　　　　　それでも感じたがっている　　　「旬」の感覚を

There are two reasons / for this. / First, / it is easier / to get good food /
２つの理由がある　　　　これには　　第１に　　より簡単である　品質のよい食べ物を手に入れることが

in its best season. / For example, / they don't need / much money /
最適な季節に　　　　　　例えば　　　　彼らは必要としない　　　多くのお金を

to buy good spinach / in winter. / Second, / they can get /
おいしいホウレンソウを買うために　　　冬に　　　第２に　　　彼らは得ることができる

a sense of the season. / Just like some birds and flowers, / bamboo shoots /
季節感を　　　　　　　　　ちょうど鳥や花のように　　　　　タケノコは

can tell Japanese people / that spring has come.
日本人に教えることができる　　　　春が来たことを

Listen & Write! (前ページの解答)

　　　"Season" is a very important word to Japanese people. They (**often**) use this word when they talk about food. They think each Japanese food has its (**best**) season. They call it "shun" in Japanese. For example, many bamboo shoots grow in spring. Japanese people can get a lot of good new bamboo shoots at this time. So, they think spring is the best season for this food.

　　　Today, it is not easy for Japanese people to (**feel**) the sense of "shun," because there are many kinds of food they can get in all four seasons. Spinach is one of these kinds of food. There are not many people who know winter is the best season for spinach, because people can get spinach in other seasons.

　　　Many Japanese people still want to feel the sense of "shun." There are two reasons for this. First, it is easier to get good food in its best season. For example, they don't (**need**) much money to buy good spinach in winter. Second, they can get a sense of the season. Just like some birds and flowers, bamboo shoots can tell Japanese people that spring (**has**) come.

Unit 23

Unit 24

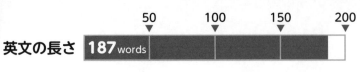

英文の長さ **187** words

	50	100	150	200

読む時間 目標 **3分7秒**

解く時間 **5分**

1回目	2回目	3回目
———	———	———

 ## *Let's read!*

次の英文は，英語の授業で，タロウ（Taro）が行ったスピーチです。これを読んで，あとの設問に答えなさい。

"Clean your room." "OK." "Let's go to the park." "OK."

This word, "OK," is often used in America and Japan. But I didn't know where the word came from. Do you know? Here are some stories I read on the Internet about it.

5 　　A long time ago, there was a president in America. His assistants came to his room and they showed him some good ideas. He looked at these ideas every day. When he liked an idea, he wrote "All Correct" on the paper. But he sometimes made spelling mistakes. He wrote "Oll Korrect," not "All 10 Correct." Then "Oll Korrect" became "OK." A newspaper used this new word "OK." Then people liked the word and began to use it too. "OK" became very popular among the people in America.

　　This is the story that I like the best about the word "OK." 15 Another story says it came from the name of a town near New York City. And another story says it came from a foreign language.

　　I don't know which story is true, but each story is interesting to me. Don't you think so too?

（青森県 改）

（注）came from 〜：〜に由来した　　president：大統領　　assistants：部下たち
All Correct：よろしい　　made spelling mistakes：つづりを間違えた
newspaper：新聞　　another story says 〜：他の話によれば〜　　true：真実の

Questions

問1　本文の内容と合っているものを，下の1〜5の中から2つ選びなさい。

   1.　タロウはOKという言葉の由来を，インターネットで読む前から知っていた。

   2.　アメリカのある大統領は，All Correctと書くところを，ときどきOll Korrectと書いた。

   3.　人々がOKという言葉を使い始め，やがて新聞も使うようになった。

   4.　OKという言葉は，ニューヨーク市という都市の名前に由来しているという話がある。

   5.　OKという言葉は，外国語に由来しているという話がある。

問2　本文の内容と合うように，下の1〜3の質問に対する答えをそれぞれ英文で書きなさい。

   1.　What countries is "OK" often used in?

   2.　What did the president's assistants do when they came to the president's room?

   3.　Did Taro talk about three stories about "OK"?

解答欄

問1			
問2	1		
	2		
	3		

Answers

答えをチェックしましょう。

問1		2，5	
問2	1	It is often used in America and Japan [In America and Japan.] .	
	2	They showed him [the president] some good ideas.	
	3	Yes, he did.	

問1 選択肢の正解，不正解の理由は次のとおりです。

× 1 2～4行目に「私はこの言葉がどこから来たのか知らなかった。それ（OK という言葉）に関して，インターネットで読んだいくつかの話がある」とあり，5行目以降で OK に関する話が述べられていることから，インターネットで読む前は知らなかったとわかります。

○ 2 8行目の But で始まる文とその次の文がヒント。英語では，あとに続く文が，前の文に説明を加える働きをすることがあります。ここでは，「だが彼はときどきつづりを間違えた。（どのように間違えたかというと，）彼は『All Correct』ではなく，『Oll Korrect』と書いたのだ」とあるので正解です。

× 3 10～12行目に「ある新聞がこの『OK』という新しい言葉を使った。その後，人々がこの言葉を気に入り，使い始めた」とあるので，「人々→新聞」ではなく「新聞→人々」の順番で伝わったことがわかります。

× 4 15～16行目に「また別の話では，ニューヨーク市の近くの町の名前に由来しているのだという」とあるので，ニューヨーク市とは違う町の名前に由来していることがわかります。

○ 5 16～17行目に「また別の話では，外国語に由来しているのだという」とあるので，正解になります。

問2 1. 2行目から America と Japan でよく使われていることがわかります。英語で答える場合は，本文に書かれている文を使うと簡単に答えることができます。ただし，代名詞に直せるものは必ず代名詞にすることを忘れないようにしましょう。

〈問題文の和訳〉「『OK』がよく使われているのはどの国々ですか」

2. 6行目に they showed him some good ideas（すばらしい提案をいくつか示した）とあります。ここでの they は the president's assistants を指し，him は the president のことです。なお，show はこのように show A B（A に B を示す）のように使われます。

〈問題文の和訳〉「大統領の部屋にやってきたとき，大統領の部下たちは何をしましたか」

3. Did で始まる疑問文なので，Yes・No で答える問題です。5～13行目の内容から①大統領のつづり間違い説，15～16行目から②ニューヨーク市の近くの町の名前説，16～17行目から③外国語説という，3つの説をタロウが話したことがわかります。

〈問題文の和訳〉「タロウは『OK』に関する3つの話をしましたか」

Vocabulary

単語と意味を確認しましょう。

☐ clean	[klíːn]	【動】きれいにする
☐ Let's …		【熟】…しよう
☐ park	[páːrk]	【名】公園
☐ America	[əmérikə]	【名】アメリカ
☐ Japan	[dʒəpǽn]	【名】日本
☐ know	[nóu]	【動】知っている
☐ where	[hwéər]	【副】どこ (に)
☐ Here is [are]〜.		【熟】〜がある。
☐ story	[stɔ́ːri]	【名】話
☐ read	[réd]	【動】read [ríːd](読む) の過去・過去分詞形
☐ a long time ago		【熟】ずっと昔に
☐ show	[ʃóu]	【動】示す
☐ idea	[aidíːə]	【名】考え, 提案
☐ look at 〜		【熟】〜を見る
☐ every day		【熟】毎日
☐ when …	[hwén]	【接】… (する) ときに
☐ like	[láik]	【動】気に入る
☐ wrote	[róut]	【動】write (書く) の過去形

☐ sometimes	[sʌ́mtàimz]	【副】ときどき
☐ then	[ðén]	【副】それから, その後
☐ became	[bikéim]	【動】become (〜になる) の過去形
☐ people	[píːpəl]	【名】人々
☐ began	[bigǽn]	【動】begin (始める) の過去形
☐ too	[túː]	【副】…もまた
☐ popular	[pápjələr]	【形】流行している, 人気がある
☐ among 〜	[əmʌ́ŋ]	【前】〜の間で
☐ say 〜	[séi]	【動】〜と言う, 〜と書いてある
☐ near 〜	[níər]	【前】〜の近くに[の]
☐ foreign language		【名】外国語
☐ each	[íːtʃ]	【形】それぞれの, どの〜も
☐ interesting	[íntərəstiŋ]	【形】おもしろい
☐ so	[sóu]	【副】そのように

和訳例

「部屋をきれいにしなさい」「OK (わかりました)」「公園に行こう」「OK (いいよ)」

この「OK」という言葉はアメリカと日本でよく使われる。しかし, 私はこの言葉がどこから来たのか知らなかった。あなたは知っているだろうか。それに関して, インターネットで私が読んだいくつかの話がある。

昔, アメリカにある大統領がいた。彼の部下たちが彼の部屋にやってきて, すばらしい提案をいくつか示した。彼はこれらの提案を毎日見た。彼はある提案が気に入ったとき, 書類に「All Correct (よろしい)」と書いた。だが彼はときどきつづりを間違えた。彼は「All Correct」ではなく「Oll Korrect」と書いたのだ。それで「Oll Korrect」が「OK」となった。ある新聞がこの「OK」という新しい言葉を使った。その後, 人々がこの言葉を気に入り, 使い始めた。「OK」はアメリカ人の間でとても人気になった。

これは「OK」という言葉に関して私が一番好きな話だ。別の話では, ニューヨーク市の近くの町の名前に由来しているのだという。また別の話では, 外国語に由来しているのだという。

私にはどの話が正しいのかわからないが, どの話も私にはおもしろい。あなたもそう思いませんか。

Unit 24

Listen & Write!

ディクテーションにチャレンジしましょう！

"Clean your room." "OK." "Let's go to the park." "OK."

This word, "OK," is often used in America and Japan.

But I didn't know where the word (　　　　　　　)

(　　　　　　　). Do you know? Here are some stories I

5 read on the Internet about it.

A long time ago, there was a president in America. His assistants came to his room and they showed him some good ideas. He looked at these ideas every day. When he liked an idea, he wrote "All Correct" on the paper. But he sometimes

10 made spelling (　　　　　　　). He wrote "Oll Korrect," not "All Correct." Then "Oll Korrect" became "OK." A newspaper used this new word "OK." Then people liked the word and began to use it too. "OK" became very popular (　　　　　　　) the people in America.

15 This is the story that I like (　　　　　　　)

(　　　　　　　) about the word "OK." Another story says it came from the name of a town near New York City. And another story says it came from a foreign language.

I don't know which story is (　　　　　　　), but each

20 story is interesting to me. Don't you think so too?

Read aloud!

音読しましょう！

"Clean your room." / "OK." / "Let's go to the park." / "OK." /
「部屋をきれいにしなさい」「OK（わかりました）」　　「公園に行こう」　　「OK（いいよ）」

This word, / "OK," / is often used / in America and Japan. / But /
この言葉　　「OK」は　　よく使われる　　アメリカと日本で　　しかし

I didn't know / where the word / came from. / Do you know? / Here are /
私は知らなかった　　どこからこの言葉が　　来たのかを　　あなたは知っているだろうか　　ある

some stories / I read / on the Internet / about it. /
いくつかの話が　私が読んだ　インターネットで　それに関して

A long time ago, / there was a president / in America. / His assistants /
昔　　　ある大統領がいた　　　　アメリカに　　彼の部下たちが

came to his room / and they showed him / some good ideas. / He looked at
彼の部屋へやってきた　　そして彼らは彼に示した　　いくつかのすばらしい提案を　彼はこれらの提案を見た

these ideas / every day. / When he liked an idea, / he wrote "All Correct" /
これらの提案を　　毎日　　彼はある提案が気に入ったとき　彼は「All Correct（よろしい）」と書いた

on the paper. / But he sometimes / made spelling mistakes. / He wrote / "Oll
書類に　　　　だが彼はときどき　　　つづりを間違えた　　彼は書いた　　「Oll

Korrect," / not "All Correct." / Then "Oll Korrect" / became "OK." / A newspaper /
「Oll Korrect」と　「All Correct」ではなく　それで「Oll Korrect」が　「OK」となった　　ある新聞が

used this new word / "OK." / Then people liked the word / and began to use it
この新しい言葉を使った　「OK」という　その後，人々はこの言葉を気に入った　そしてそれを使い始めた

too. / "OK" became / very popular / among the people / in America. /
もまた　「OK」はなった　とても人気に　　人々の間で　　　アメリカの

This is the story / that I like the best / about the word / "OK." /
これは話である　　私が一番好きな　　その言葉に関して　「OK」という

Another story says / it came from the name / of a town / near New York City. /
別の話はいう　　　それは名前に由来した　　町の　　ニューヨーク市の近くの

And another story says / it came from / a foreign language. /
また別の話はいう　　　それは由来した　　外国語に

I don't know / which story is true, / but each story / is interesting / to me. /
私にはわからない　　どの話が正しいのか　　だが，どの話も　　おもしろい　　私には

Don't you think so / too?
あなたはそう思いませんか　　もまた

Listen & Write! （前ページの解答）

"Clean your room." "OK." "Let's go to the park." "OK."
This word, "OK," is often used in America and Japan. But I didn't know where the word (came)
(from). Do you know? Here are some stories I read on the Internet about it.
A long time ago, there was a president in America. His assistants came to his room and they showed
him some good ideas. He looked at these ideas every day. When he liked an idea, he wrote "All Correct"
on the paper. But he sometimes made spelling (mistakes). He wrote "Oll Korrect," not "All Correct."
Then "Oll Korrect" became "OK." A newspaper used this new word "OK." Then people liked the word
and began to use it too. "OK" became very popular (among) the people in America.
This is the story that I like (the) (best) about the word "OK." Another story says it came
from the name of a town near New York City. And another story says it came from a foreign language.
I don't know which story is (true), but each story is interesting to me. Don't you think so too?

Unit 24

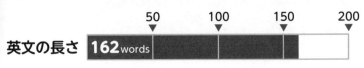

Unit 25

英文の長さ **162** words

| 50 | 100 | 150 | 200 |

📖 読む時間　目標　**2分42秒**

✏️ 解く時間　　　**2分**

1回目 ——————　2回目 ——————　3回目 ——————

Let's read!

次の英文を読んで，あとの設問に答えなさい。

Mike : Lucy, are you (1) next Sunday?

Lucy : Well, I'm going to go shopping with my mother. Why?

Mike : I'm going to see a movie with Mary and John. We want you to join us.

5 Lucy : Oh, I see. Will you tell me about the movie?

Mike : O.K. It's an exciting movie and Tom Cruise is in it.

Lucy : Tom Cruise! I like him very much. I want to see it. What time does it start?

Mike : It starts at ten in the morning.

10 Lucy : What time does it end?

Mike : Well, the movie is two hours and thirty minutes long, so (2)

Lucy : Oh, I see. Then, I think I can go shopping in the afternoon. I'll ask my mother.

15 Mike : That's good. Mary and John will be happy to see you.

Lucy : What time shall we meet?

Mike : How about nine thirty? I'll meet you in front of the movie theater.

Lucy : O.K. See you then.

(三重県)

(注) go shopping：買い物に行く　　exciting：ワクワクする
Tom Cruise：トム・クルーズ（アメリカの俳優）　　end：終わる　　in front of 〜：〜の前で
the movie theater：映画館

152

Questions

問1 空所 (1) に入れるのに最も適切な語をア〜エの中から選びなさい。

ア．sure　イ．busy　ウ．fine　エ．glad

問2 空所 (2) に入れるのに最も適切な英文をア〜エの中から選びなさい。

ア．it ends at eleven.　　イ．it ends at eleven thirty.
ウ．it ends at twelve.　　エ．it ends at twelve thirty.

解答欄

問1		問2	

Answers

答えをチェックしましょう。

問1	イ	問2	エ

問1　空所の次のルーシーの発言がヒント。マイクの「ルーシー，今度の日曜は（　　　）かい？」に対して，「そうね，母と一緒に買い物に行く予定よ。どうして？」と返事をしているので，日曜日に予定があるかどうかを尋ねていることがわかります。空所には busy（忙しい）か free（ひまな）が入ると考えられますが，選択肢には busy しかないのでイが正解になります。

〈選択肢の和訳〉
　　× ア. 確かな
　　○ イ. 忙しい
　　× ウ. 元気な
　　× エ. うれしい

問2　空所の3行前からの発言がヒント。「それは午前 10 時に始まるよ」「それは何時に終わるの？」に対して，「ええと，その映画は 2 時間 30 分の長さだから（　　　）」と返事をしています。したがって，空所に入る終了時刻は「10 時＋ 2 時間 30 分＝ 12 時 30 分」となり，エが正解とわかります。

〈選択肢の和訳〉
　　× ア. それは 11 時に終わります。
　　× イ. それは 11 時 30 分に終わります。
　　× ウ. それは 12 時に終わります。
　　○ エ. それは 12 時 30 分に終わります。

重要な表現⑪

want＋人＋to 不定詞は「人に…してほしい」

マイクの2番目のセリフ，**We want <u>you</u> to join us.**（僕たちは<u>君</u>に加わってほしいんだ）は，「動詞＋<u>人</u>＋to 不定詞」の語順で使われ，「<u>人</u>に…してほしい」という意味を表します（→p. 112）。want to ...（…したい）との違いに注意して覚えておきましょう。

I want <u>you</u> to go there.

（私は<u>あなたに</u>そこに行ってほしい）　　→「行く」のは you「あなた」

I want to go there. （私はそこに行きたい）　　→「行く」のは I「私」

154

Vocabulary

単語と意味を確認しましょう。

☐ busy	[bízi]	【形】忙しい	
☐ next	[nékst]	【形】次の	
☐ Sunday	[sʌ́ndei]	【名】日曜日	
☐ be going to ...		【熟】…するつもりである	
☐ mother	[mʌ́ðər]	【名】母	
☐ why	[hwái]	【副】なぜ, どうして	
☐ see	[síː]	【動】見る, わかる, 会う	
☐ movie	[múːvi]	【名】映画	
☐ want ～ to ...		【熟】～に…してほしい	
☐ join	[dʒɔ́in]	【動】加わる, 参加する	
☐ tell	[tél]	【動】話す	
☐ like	[láik]	【動】好きである	
☐ want to ...		【熟】…したい	

☐ start	[stáːrt]	【動】始まる	
☐ in the morning		【熟】午前中の [に]	
☐ long	[lɔ́(ː)ŋ]	【形】～の長さだ	
☐ so ...	[sóu]	【接】だから…	
☐ think	[θíŋk]	【動】思う, 考える	
☐ can ...	[kən]	【助】…できる	
☐ in the afternoon		【熟】午後の [に]	
☐ ask	[ǽsk]	【動】尋ねる	
☐ happy to ...		【熟】…して [できて] うれしい	
☐ shall we [I] ...?		【熟】…しましょうか	
☐ meet	[míːt]	【動】会う	
☐ How about ～ ?		【熟】～はどうですか。	

和訳例

Mike：ルーシー，今度の日曜は忙しいかい？

Lucy：そうね，母と一緒に買い物に行く予定よ。どうして？

Mike：僕はメアリーとジョンと一緒に映画を見に行く予定なんだ。僕たちは君に加わってほしいんだ。

Lucy：まあ，わかったわ。その映画について教えてくれないかしら。

Mike：いいよ。ワクワクする映画で，トム・クルーズが出演しているんだ。

Lucy：トム・クルーズですって！　私は彼がとても好きなの。その映画見たいわ。それは何時に始まるの？

Mike：それは午前10時に始まるよ。

Lucy：それは何時に終わるの？

Mike：ええと，その映画は2時間30分の長さだから，12時30分に終わるよ。

Lucy：ああ，わかったわ。じゃあ，買い物は午後に行けると思うわ。母に聞いてみるわね。

Mike：それはよかった。メアリーとジョンは君に会えてうれしいだろう。

Lucy：何時に会いましょうか。

Mike：9時30分はどうかな。映画館の前で会おう。

Lucy：わかったわ。そのときに会いましょう。

Unit 25

Listen & Write!
ディクテーションにチャレンジしましょう！

Mike : Lucy, are you busy next Sunday?

Lucy : Well, I'm going to go shopping with my mother. Why?

Mike : I'm going to see a movie with Mary and John. We want

you to (   ) us.

5 Lucy : Oh, I see. Will you tell me about the movie?

Mike : O.K. It's an exciting movie and Tom Cruise is

(   ) (   ).

Lucy : Tom Cruise! I like him very much. I want to see it.

What time does it start?

10 Mike : It starts at ten in the morning.

Lucy : What time does it end?

Mike : Well, the movie is two hours and thirty minutes

(   ), so it ends at twelve thirty.

Lucy : Oh, I see. Then, I think I can go shopping in the

15   afternoon. I'll ask my mother.

Mike : That's good. Mary and John will be happy to see you.

Lucy : What time (   ) we meet?

Mike : (   ) (   ) nine thirty? I'll

meet you in front of the movie theater.

20 Lucy : O.K. See you then.

Read aloud!

音読しましょう！

Mike : Lucy, / are you busy / next Sunday? /
　　　　ルーシー　　　忙しいかい　　　　　今度の日曜

Lucy : Well, / I'm going to go shopping / with my mother. / Why? /
　　　　そうね　　　　買い物に行く予定よ　　　　母と一緒に　　　　　どうして

Mike : I'm going to see a movie / with Mary and John. / We want you /
　　　　僕は映画を見に行く予定なんだ　　　　メアリーとジョンと一緒に　　　　僕たちは君にしてほしい

　　　　to join us. /
　　　　僕たちに加わることを

Lucy : Oh, I see. / Will you tell me / about the movie? /
　　　　まあ, わかったわ　　教えてくれないかしら　　　その映画について

Mike : O.K. / It's an exciting movie / and Tom Cruise / is in it. /
　　　　いいよ　　それはワクワクする映画なんだ　　　そしてトム・クルーズが　出演しているんだ

Lucy : Tom Cruise! / I like him / very much. / I want / to see it. / What time /
　　　　トム・クルーズ！　私は彼が好きなの　　とても　　　私はしたい　それを見ることを　　　何時に

　　　　does it start? /
　　　　それは始まるの？

Mike : It starts / at ten / in the morning. /
　　　　それは始まる　10時に　　　　午前

Lucy : What time / does it end? /
　　　　何時に　　　それは終わるの

Mike : Well, / the movie is / two hours / and thirty minutes long, / so it ends /
　　　　ええと　　その映画は　　2時間　　　と30分の長さだ　　　だからそれは終わる

　　　　at twelve thirty. /
　　　　12時30分に

Lucy : Oh, I see. / Then, / I think / I can go shopping / in the afternoon. /
　　　　ああ, わかったわ　　じゃあ　私は思う　私は買い物に行けると　　　　午後に

　　　　I'll ask / my mother. /
　　　　私は聞いてみる　母に

Mike : That's good. / Mary and John / will be happy / to see you. /
　　　　それはよかった　　メアリーとジョンは　　うれしいだろう　　君に会えて

Lucy : What time / shall we meet? /
　　　　何時に　　　会いましょうか

Mike : How about / nine thirty? / I'll meet you / in front of the movie theater. /
　　　　どうかな　　9時30分では　　僕は君に会おう　　　映画館の前で

Lucy : O.K. / See you then.
　　　　わかった　では, そのときに会いましょう

Listen & Write! （前ページの解答）

Mike : Lucy, are you busy next Sunday?
Lucy : Well, I'm going to go shopping with my mother. Why?
Mike : I'm going to see a movie with Mary and John. We want you to (**join**) us.
Lucy : Oh, I see. Will you tell me about the movie?
Mike : O.K. It's an exciting movie and Tom Cruise is (**in**) (**it**).
Lucy : Tom Cruise! I like him very much. I want to see it. What time does it start?
Mike : It starts at ten in the morning.
Lucy : What time does it end?
Mike : Well, the movie is two hours and thirty minutes (**long**), so it ends at twelve thirty.
Lucy : Oh, I see. Then, I think I can go shopping in the afternoon. I'll ask my mother.
Mike : That's good. Mary and John will be happy to see you.
Lucy : What time (**shall**) we meet?
Mike : (**How**) (**about**) nine thirty? I'll meet you in front of the movie theater.
Lucy : O.K. See you then.

Unit 25

不規則動詞活用表

	原形	過去形	過去分詞形	意味
A-A-A型（原形・過去形・過去分形とも同じ形）	☐ cost	☐ cost	☐ cost	（費用が）かかる
	☐ cut	☐ cut	☐ cut	切る
	☐ hit	☐ hit	☐ hit	打つ
	☐ hurt	☐ hurt	☐ hurt	傷つける
	☐ let	☐ let	☐ let	させる
	☐ put	☐ put	☐ put	置く
	☐ set	☐ set	☐ set	配置する
	☐ shut	☐ shut	☐ shut	閉める
	☐ spread	☐ spread	☐ spread	広げる
A-B-B型（過去形と過去分形が同じ形）	☐ bring	☐ brought	☐ brought	持ってくる
	☐ build	☐ built	☐ built	建てる
	☐ burn	☐ burnt	☐ burnt	焼く
	☐ buy	☐ bought	☐ bought	買う
	☐ catch	☐ caught	☐ caught	捕まえる
	☐ feel	☐ felt	☐ felt	感じる
	☐ fight	☐ fought	☐ fought	戦う
	☐ find	☐ found	☐ found	見つける
	☐ hang	☐ hung	☐ hung	つるす
	☐ have	☐ had	☐ had	持つ
	☐ hear	☐ heard	☐ heard	聞く
	☐ hold	☐ held	☐ held	抱く
	☐ keep	☐ kept	☐ kept	保つ
	☐ lay	☐ laid	☐ laid	横たえる
	☐ lead	☐ led	☐ led	導く
	☐ leave	☐ left	☐ left	去る
	☐ lend	☐ lent	☐ lent	貸す
	☐ lose	☐ lost	☐ lost	失う
	☐ make	☐ made	☐ made	作る

	原形	過去形	過去分詞形	意味
A-B-B型 (過去形と過去分詞形が同じ形)	☐ mean	☐ meant	☐ meant	意味する
	☐ meet	☐ met	☐ met	会う
	☐ pay	☐ paid	☐ paid	支払う
	☐ read [ríːd]	☐ read [réd]	☐ read [réd]	読む
	☐ say	☐ said	☐ said	言う
	☐ sell	☐ sold	☐ sold	売る
	☐ send	☐ sent	☐ sent	送る
	☐ shine	☐ shone	☐ shone	輝く
	☐ shoot	☐ shot	☐ shot	撃つ
	☐ sit	☐ sat	☐ sat	座る
	☐ sleep	☐ slept	☐ slept	眠る
	☐ spend	☐ spent	☐ spent	費やす
	☐ stand	☐ stood	☐ stood	立つ
	☐ teach	☐ taught	☐ taught	教える
	☐ tell	☐ told	☐ told	言う
	☐ think	☐ thought	☐ thought	考える
	☐ understand	☐ understood	☐ understood	理解する
	☐ win	☐ won	☐ won	勝つ
A-B-A型 (原形と過去分詞形が同じ形)	☐ become	☐ became	☐ become	(〜に) なる
	☐ come	☐ came	☐ come	来る
	☐ run	☐ ran	☐ run	走る
A-B-C型 (原形・過去形・過去分詞形が3つとも違う形)	☐ begin	☐ began	☐ begun	始める
	☐ blow	☐ blew	☐ blown	吹く
	☐ break	☐ broke	☐ broken	壊す
	☐ choose	☐ chose	☐ chosen	選ぶ
	☐ do	☐ did	☐ done	する
	☐ draw	☐ drew	☐ drawn	引く
	☐ drink	☐ drank	☐ drunk	飲む
	☐ drive	☐ drove	☐ driven	運転する
	☐ eat	☐ ate	☐ eaten	食べる

	原形	過去形	過去分詞形	意味
A-B-C型（原形・過去形・過去分詞形が３つとも違う形）	☐ fall	☐ fell	☐ fallen	落ちる
	☐ fly	☐ flew	☐ flown	飛ぶ
	☐ forget	☐ forgot	☐ forgotten /forgot	忘れる
	☐ forgive	☐ forgave	☐ forgiven	許す
	☐ freeze	☐ froze	☐ frozen	凍る
	☐ get	☐ got	☐ gotten/got	得る
	☐ give	☐ gave	☐ given	与える
	☐ go	☐ went	☐ gone	行く
	☐ grow	☐ grew	☐ grown	成長する
	☐ know	☐ knew	☐ known	知る
	☐ lie	☐ lay	☐ lain	横たわる
	☐ ride	☐ rode	☐ ridden	乗る
	☐ ring	☐ rang	☐ rung	鳴る
	☐ rise	☐ rose	☐ risen	昇る
	☐ see	☐ saw	☐ seen	見る
	☐ sing	☐ sang	☐ sung	歌う
	☐ speak	☐ spoke	☐ spoken	話す
	☐ strike	☐ struck	☐ striken /struck	打つ
	☐ swim	☐ swam	☐ swum	泳ぐ
	☐ take	☐ took	☐ taken	取る
	☐ throw	☐ threw	☐ thrown	投げる
	☐ wake	☐ woke	☐ woken	目覚める
	☐ wear	☐ wore	☐ worn	着ている
	☐ write	☐ wrote	☐ written	書く

大岩 秀樹

東進ハイスクール中等部・東進中学 NET 講師。23 歳で衛星放送を通じて全国配信される授業の担当講師に大抜擢され，現在は中学生〜大学生・社会人を対象とする数多くの講座を担当。基礎・応用・入試対策講座などを幅広く担当し，高校入試だけでなく，大学入試やその先まで視野に入れた授業に定評がある。著書（含共著）は『中学英語レベル別問題集』シリーズ（東進ブックス），『短期で攻める　1 日 1 題 1 週間　スピード英語長文』シリーズ（桐原書店）など多数。

安河内 哲也

東進ハイスクール・東進ビジネススクール講師。各種教育関連機関での講演活動を通じて実用英語教育の普及活動をしている。わかりやすい授業や参考書で定評がある。著者（含共著）は『短期で攻める　1 日 1 題 1 週間　スピード英語長文』シリーズ，『大学入試　英語長文　ハイパートレーニング』シリーズ（共に桐原書店）など多数。

● **英文校閲**　Karl Matsumoto
● **編集協力**　小宮 徹／山越 友子

桐原書店の
デジタル学習サービス

ハイパー英語教室
中学英語長文2　改訂版 [入試長文がすらすら読める編]

2012 年 6 月 30 日　初　版第 1 刷発行
2020 年 10 月 10 日　初　版第 11 刷発行
2021 年 7 月 15 日　改訂版第 1 刷発行
2024 年 8 月 10 日　改訂版第 5 刷発行

著　者　　　　　大岩 秀樹／安河内 哲也
発行人　　　　　門間 正哉
発行所　　　　　株式会社 桐原書店
　　　　　　　　〒 114-0001
　　　　　　　　東京都北区東十条3-10-36
　　　　　　　　TEL：03-5302-7010（販売）
　　　　　　　　www.kirihara.co.jp
装丁　　　　　　徳永 裕美
レイアウト　　　新田 由起子（ムーブ）／徳永 裕美
イラスト（キャラクターデザイン）　坂崎 千春
イラスト　　　　オカムラ ナオミ
DTP　　　　　　徳永 裕美
印刷・製本　　　TOPPANクロレ株式会社

重要な発音記号Best15

発音記号は単語の発音の仕方を示す記号です。単語集などについているカタカナはあくまでも参考で，英語の正しい発音とは異なります。最初は難しく感じるかもしれませんが，ネイティブスピーカーの音声などを使いながら少しずつ発音記号を覚えて，正しい英語の発音を身につけていきましょう。

声に出して読んでみましょう。

□	1	[ɑ]	口を大きく開いて，ノドの奥から響かせて発音する「ア」。	□ **b**o**dy** [bɑ́di] 体 □ **st**o**p** [stɑ́p] 止まる

□ 1 [ɑ]　口を大きく開いて，ノドの奥から響かせて発音する「ア」。
　□ **b**o**dy** [bɑ́di]　体
　□ **st**o**p** [stɑ́p]　止まる

□ 2 [æ]　「エーアー」と発音し，音が切り替わるときの「エ」と「ア」の中間音。口の両端を横に強く広げる。
　□ **c**a**t** [kǽt]　ネコ
　□ **h**a**ppy** [hǽpi]　うれしい

□ 3 [ʌ]　口をあまり開かず，ノドの奥で短く，低く発音する「ア」。
　□ **b**u**s** [bʌ́s]　バス
　□ **c**u**t** [kʌ́t]　切る

□ 4 [ə]　口は半開き，口の真ん中で力を抜き，低くあいまいに発音する「ア」。
　□ **a**bout [əbáut]　～について
　□ **a**lone [əlóun]　ひとりで

□ 5 [ɔː]　口を上下縦長に開いて，低い音で長く発音する「オー」。
　□ **A**ugust [ɔ́ːgəst]　8月
　□ **b**a**ll** [bɔ́ːl]　ボール

□ 6 [ɑː]　日本語の「アー」とほぼ同じ音だが，より大きく口とノドを開けて発音する。
　□ **f**a**ther** [fɑ́ːðər]　父
　□ **p**a**lm** [pɑ́ːm]　ヤシ